Praise for
Mother-Daughter Duet

"The special bond between mothers and daughters doesn't have to vanish as our daughters leave the nest. Written with honesty, insight, and love, Cheri Fuller and Ali Plum take turns giving inspiring advice and practical tips on how mothers and daughters can forge an alliance that offers meaningful gifts to each other. This sweet book will be a wonderful bridge between mothers and their adult daughters."

—SHARON HERSH, author of *The Last Addiction* and
    Bravehearts

"Got conflict? Cheri Fuller and Ali Plum have a book that will help you understand the challenges and transitions of the mother-daughter relationship. With meticulous research, personal vulnerability, and 'right-on' wisdom, they reveal tools that bring resolution, understanding, and transformation to complicated relationships. Don't be surprised if you recognize a version of your own story in this not-to-be-missed book. You'll find answers that produce positive results."

—CAROL KENT, speaker and author of *When I Lay My
    Isaac Down*

"*Mother-Daughter Duet* is a wonderful book, a story told from the heart, full of ideas on how to connect in loving, healthy ways with our daughters and even our daughters-in-law."

—JENNIFER ROTHSCHILD, speaker and author of *Lessons I
    Learned in the Dark*

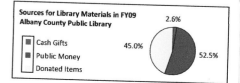

"We shared *Mother-Daughter Duet* around our office, and we all gained help and hope for relationships with daughters, daughters-in-law, and our own mothers! Thanks for a very honest practical read."

—PAM FARREL, relationship specialist, international speaker, and author of more than thirty books

"Disarmingly honest and inspiring, this amazing book will become your trusted guide through the mysterious waters in your own mother-daughter relationship. If you've ever been tempted to drive four hundred miles to take your sad daughter to lunch, or felt the need to escape your mom's presence abruptly, or hide dark emotions from an overly concerned mom, you'll love the honest insights in the section, 'A Daughter's Perspective.' This book will bring hope for now and help for the uncharted relational territory to come."

—LESLIE PARROTT, founder of Realrelationships.com and author of *You Matter More Than You Think.*

"*Mother-Daughter Duet* is a helpful and wise resource for those struggling with mother-daughter relationship issues. I gleaned some great tips that will help me be a better friend to my adult daughter."

—LESLIE VERNICK, licensed counselor, speaker, and author of *Lord, I Just Want to be Happy* and *The Emotionally Destructive Relationship*

MOTHER-DAUGHTER Duet

CHERI FULLER & ALI PLUM

MOTHER-DAUGHTER Duet

Getting to the Relationship You Want with Your Adult Daughter

MULTNOMAH
BOOKS

MOTHER-DAUGHTER DUET
PUBLISHED BY MULTNOMAH BOOKS
12265 Oracle Boulevard, Suite 200
Colorado Springs, Colorado 80921

All Scripture quotations and paraphrases, unless otherwise indicated, are taken from the *Holy Bible, New International Version*®. NIV®. Copyright © 1973, 1978, 1984 by International Bible Society. Used by permission of Zondervan Publishing House. All rights reserved. Scripture quotations marked (MSG) are taken from The Message by Eugene H. Peterson. Copyright © 1993, 1994, 1995, 1996, 2000, 2001, 2002. Used by permission of NavPress Publishing Group. All rights reserved. Scripture quotations marked (NLT) are taken from the Holy Bible, New Living Translation, copyright © 2004. Used by permission of Tyndale House Publishers Inc., Wheaton, Illinois 60189. All rights reserved.

Details in some anecdotes and stories have been changed to protect the identities of the persons involved.

ISBN 978-1-60142-162-3
ISBN 978-1-60142-163-0 (electronic)

Copyright © 2010 by Cheri Fuller and Ali D. Plum

Published in association with the literary agency of Alive Communications Inc., 7680 Goddard Street, Suite 200, Colorado Springs, CO 80920, www.alivecommunications.com.

Published in the United States by WaterBrook Multnomah, an imprint of the Crown Publishing Group, a division of Random House Inc., New York.

MULTNOMAH and its mountain colophon are registered trademarks of Random House Inc.

Library of Congress Cataloging-in-Publication Data
Fuller, Cheri.
    Mother-daughter duet : getting to the relationship you want with your adult daughter / Cheri Fuller and Ali Plum.
        p. cm.
    ISBN 978-1-60142-162-3—ISBN 978-1-60142-163-0 (electronic) 1. Mothers and daughters. 2. Daughters—Psychology. 3. Parent and adult child. 4. Adult children—Family relationships. I. Plum, Ali. II. Title.
    HQ755.86.F854 2010
    306.874'3—dc22

                              2009035677

Printed in the United States of America
2010—First Edition

10 9 8 7 6 5 4 3 2 1

SPECIAL SALES

Most WaterBrook Multnomah books are available at special quantity discounts when purchased in bulk by corporations, organizations, and special-interest groups. Custom imprinting or excerpting can also be done to fit special needs. For information, please e-mail SpecialMarkets@WaterBrookMultnomah.com or call 1-800-603-7051.

CONTENTS

MOTHER-DAUGHTER

AN INTRICATE DUET

• • • • •

We all hope to feel our mother's arm around our shoulders when we're worried, to feel it gently let go when life calms down. It's an intricate duet that moms and daughters dance—one backing off when the other needs space, moving up close when the unfamiliar threatens.

—CATHIE KRYCZKA, WWW.TODAYSPARENT.COM

• • • • •

One late afternoon seven years ago, I took care of my daughter's baby and toddler boys while she went to the doctor. I walked around the house, holding four-month-old Luke in my arms, patting his little back and singing to him to help his colic. Today he's a healthy seven-year-old, but those were stressful months—and long nights of Ali being up with night-owl baby Luke. My daughter's young family lived with us at the time, so I helped whenever I could.

"Hungry, Nandy! Nuggets! Cheerios!" twenty-month-old Noah implored. Holding Luke, I raced around the kitchen, popping chicken nuggets on a cookie sheet and into the oven, then handing him a cup of Cheerios to stave off his hunger. I turned on a Barney video to entertain Noah while the chicken nuggets baked and kept patting and rocking Luke. Needless to say, after two hours this grandma was pooped!

When Ali walked in, she took Luke from me and gave him a kiss. I offered her a glass of iced tea and a muffin, and we sat down in the family room. I was hoping we could talk since Luke had simmered down a bit.

"How'd your doctor's appointment go?"

After her brief answer I said, "You know, honey, I read this week that when a nursing mom consumes citrus fruits, dairy, and even caffeine, it can cause gas in the baby. Cutting those out might help Luke cry less. What do you think?"

In seconds I knew I'd said the wrong thing.

"With Luke awake all night, how do you think I could get through the day without several cups of coffee? I can't cut out caffeine!"

Then I started trying to explain that the article had suggested she could drink black or green tea instead. Mistake number two. That just made her madder.

"You just don't understand, and you're so annoying," she said, grabbing her diaper bag. She took Noah's hand and headed for the door. "I'm going for a ride."

I was sorry to have irritated her, and I believed I was only trying to help by offering a little suggestion. No chat, no thank-yous for caring for the boys; just biting my head off and leaving.

I often had no idea what kind of mood my daughter would be in—angry or euphoric, depressed or pleasant. Occasionally we had some great moments together, but those were becoming few and far between. Many times when we were around each other, I felt I couldn't do anything right. Whenever I opened my mouth, whatever I did, no matter how loving my intention—it would irritate her. She'd be exasperated and say, "Oh Mom!" or say nothing at all.

Her resentment hurt. I felt her disdain and judgment and didn't know where it was coming from or what I'd done to deserve it. I could see she was trying to separate and be her own person, and I was trying to give her the space she needed. I was also aware of our differences, but they didn't explain her attitude toward me or the distance between us.

Time after time I was driven to God and prayer—not as a last resort but because he told us to cast our cares, concerns, and worries on him (1 Peter 5:7)—and I definitely had some concerns for my relationship with my daughter. I asked for strength and wisdom to know how to be a support to her in this transition time. I knew prayer was the greatest influence in my children's lives—especially now that they were gone from home—and I'd prayed countless prayers for her over the months and years. But nothing seemed to change in our relationship.

I just wanted my daughter back, the daughter I'd carried for nine months and held until she crawled and then learned to walk—the much-anticipated only daughter whose birth was surrounded with so much joy it was like Christmas Day although it was November. I wanted the daughter back who'd giggled as I pushed her in the swing at the park, smiled with her shining blue eyes in pictures, and loved for us to hop on our bikes and ride to Braum's for an ice cream cone. And who, after winter school days, even in her preteen and early teenage years, asked me to stop for hot cocoa and talk. I just wanted us to get along like we used to.

I loved my daughter immensely and didn't understand why as a young adult she was so angry with me and why she kept pushing me away. I gave her—and our relationship—to God so many times I can't count, yet the rift in our relationship lasted through most of her twenties.

Though I held fast to my faith during those years, I sometimes wondered, *Will we ever have harmony between us or will her attitude toward me always be laced with hostility? Is our connection forever lost? Is she always going to be annoyed with me? Will we ever enjoy each other again?* I didn't know.

THE MOTHER-DAUGHTER RELATIONSHIP: A DUET OF SHADE AND LIGHT

We aren't the only mother and daughter pair who've struggled or had tension in their relationship. It's common for a mother and daughter's interaction to be rocky during the transition from adolescence and the twenties and even through adulthood. The mom-daughter connection is an intricate, close relationship that is static and changing at the same time. It's static because of the strong bond we've had since our children's birth, and it's changing because we're human and our daughters are going through different stages of life, as we are as well. Even as our relationship spans the decades and seasons, it's a paradox, and that's why it's complicated.

Think of all the history you have with your daughter, all the bonding and good times. First birthday and first day of school. First stitches and ballet shoes. School programs, Brownie Scout meetings, and inevitable skinned knees. First pierced earrings, lipstick, heels, and dates. Graduation and all the years and laughter and tears—and arguments—in between.

The closeness of the mother-daughter bond holds much potential for conflict. Usually the conflict starts in the teenage years, if not before. When your daughter was little, she may have clip-clopped around in your red high heels and said, "Mommy, I want to be just like you when I grow up!" Yet when she arrived at adolescence, she started rolling her eyes at your advice and letting you know that she didn't want to be *anything* like you.

Sound familiar? You're not alone, but there is hope. I too found my daughter's separating-transitioning-individuating times difficult, and often baffling, as you'll read about in the pages ahead.

Yet today, about twelve years later, Ali and I have the friendship—

the mother-daughter duet—I'd hoped for. We understand each other more, accept each other, and even appreciate our differences. We have forgiven each other for many hurts and made peace with the past. Most of the time we truly enjoy each other's company and friendship. But it was not a quick process. It took a lot of work to get here. For a long while it seemed that when we were together, we clashed like a junior high school band more than we harmonized like a skilled orchestra—and there was no way we were going to sing a duet. We had no idea what a long journey it would be, but it's definitely been worth the effort.

Along the way toward figuring out why things were strained between us and getting to a healthier, more enjoyable relationship, we discovered principles you'll find woven through the stories and chapters ahead—like letting go, respecting and believing in your daughter, listening and taking care of yourself—and the powerful effect of forgiveness. All of these have helped turn our relationship around.

CONVERSATIONS WITH MOTHERS AND DAUGHTERS

Every mother and daughter has a unique story of their relationship and life. That's why Ali and I share our story as well as those of other moms and daughters of different ages and from different places. Over a period of many months, we interviewed many women. When I went to speak at a women's event in Dallas, Texas, or a rural area of Kansas, the Washington DC area, or California, I sat down and talked with women about their mother-daughter relationships: *What was the hot button or issue that brought conflict between you? What's the best way you've found to connect? What are the communication barriers—things you say that your daughter reacts to?*

If it was daughters I was talking with, I asked: *What does your mom say that makes you want to stop the conversation? What do you need from your mom? What can your mom do to help your relationship?* To moms we asked: *What's different about your daughter's and your generations? What was your relationship with your own mother like? What's a story you could tell me that shows how a turnaround happened in your mom-daughter relationship?*

Though when we started Ali intended to interview the daughters and I the moms, she ended up interviewing some insightful mothers and I learned so much from talking with daughters. In coffee shops, restaurants, and airports, in our neighborhood, church, and other cities, via e-mail and Facebook, Ali and I talked with daughters from college age to forty-something and with moms from their late thirties to their seventies. We heard what they love about each other and what hurts and annoys them, what they like to do together and how they reconciled after a period of distance—and we share many of their stories in the chapters ahead.

IS THIS BOOK FOR YOU?

Looking into the past to process what had happened in our relationship is the hardest thing either of us has ever done. But we were willing to go there because we know what it's like to come out of the struggle and conflict to relate as equals and adult friends and how enormously satisfying that is. Because of our experience, we want to provide hope for discouraged moms who think their daughters are too far gone, or for the mom who simply doesn't understand her daughter or just longs for a closer, more connected relationship.

We've heard so many women talk about their struggles and hopes in relationship to their moms or daughters. They spoke with candor and angst when it came to past and present experiences. Ali's section, "A Daughter's Perspective," is a portal to help moms better understand what their daughters might be feeling in order to gain more effective ways to relate to them. In this part of each chapter, you'll hear what your daughter might be thinking or has been trying to tell you for a long time. It's our hope that it may even produce an "aha!" moment that can empower and encourage you.

Maybe as you read our story, you'll think the issues facing you and your daughter are quite different than ours. Perhaps you get into shouting matches or exist in a cold war of silence because so many subjects are taboo, thus avoiding the issues that keep you apart. Your daughter is a woman now and thinks you're still mothering her, so she pushes you away. Or maybe your daughter knows exactly how to push your buttons and relishes doing so. Or you raised her in a good church and now she'll have nothing to do with your "religion." Perhaps your daughter has moved across the country or across the world, and you wonder if the distance in miles reflects the disconnection between you.

Whatever the specifics of your situation, maybe you are thinking, *I'm so discouraged with my adult daughter. I don't know what's wrong, but we just don't get along. We surely don't have the relationship I'd longed for.* Or perhaps, *Our connection is good but I want it to grow. And sometimes I worry about the choices she's making...* This book can help.

Regardless of your past, present, or impending future, you and your daughter can be reunited; your relationship can be more satisfying. It's never too late to find the strength that comes from forgiveness and acceptance, the peace received from understanding and empathy. We hope that through the pages ahead you'll find ways to step into your daughter's shoes, or to reflect on your relationship with your own mother, or perhaps discover glimpses of hope and encouragement if your daughter is in crisis or estranged from you.

You'll read some things we moms often unknowingly do and say that can either undermine or build the relationship. We've also tucked in countless ways to help you connect or reconnect with your adult daughter, as well as some building blocks for a lifelong friendship. Discussion Questions are added for you to gather some moms and have your own conversations about the issues in the book. There are questions for each chapter, ideal for discussion in a small group, book club, or for individual reflection.

Ali and I haven't arrived. We are two very different, imperfect women who have worked on our relationship and learned to get along and enjoy and accept each other, but not without struggle along the way. We encourage each other and often make each other laugh. Yet we still have days when we are relating in an "off-key" way. We sometimes agree and other times disagree. But we've discovered an enduring bond—a mother-daughter duet—that enriches both of our lives.

You and your daughter can too.

It starts with you, Mom, even if it seems your daughter is unwilling. You can make the first move. You can change your approach and find new ways to relate to her. And a new relationship can grow through all the seasons that are ahead for both of you.

LETTING GO

• • • • •

It was hard when you went away—
for how was I to know
The serendipity of letting go
would be seeing you come home again
and meeting in a new way
woman to woman—
friend to friend.

—MARILEE ZDENEK, *SPLINTERS IN MY PRIDE*[1]

• • • • •

The college and career years are a transitional time, whether your daughter takes a conventional route to a four-year university a state away, attends a community college, settles into a job and her own apartment, or pursues an entirely different path such as joining the Peace Corps or moving to New York for culinary school, or maybe she has a baby right out of high school or moves in with her boyfriend. For daughters, it's a journey toward individuation—that is, being able to live independently from parents. For moms, it may be a time of angst, worry *(Can she make it without me?)*, and even a sense of loss *(Where did my baby go?)*.

In the midst of these changes, a daughter needs three major components in order to live independently and become a purposeful and confident adult: a sense of belonging, a feeling of being loved and worth-while, and a sense of being capable. You provided the first two—a feeling of belonging and being worthwhile—the best you knew how as you raised her. By providing her with nurture and care from infancy throughout her growing-up years, you built the foundation for her growing sense of value and worth. Not a perfect foundation because none of us do the challenging job of raising kids flawlessly. There are no perfect parents.

But a young woman also needs the vital "capability component." She needs to become independent and see herself as a *separate entity* who has the ability to cope with life on her own and build her own relationships, career, and family *apart from her parents.* In other words, she needs a *clear sense of separation with attachment,* which means being able to feel good as a separate person while staying in relationship with her mother.

Sometimes we unwittingly derail a daughter's separation and capability component by clinging and controlling rather than letting go. Although we want her to find her true self and her purpose, some of the things we moms say and do are counterproductive to that very process.

"Do you want to create an adult baby? Then hang on to your daughter," said Marie Chapian in *Mothers and Daughters,* by reminding her you're the only one who truly loves and understands her, telling her often how you don't know how to make it without her. "Do your best to keep her needy and dependent," Chapian adds. "Put your own life on hold, and remind her regularly you don't know where she'd be without you."[2]

Like many other challenges in life, letting go of our kids is easier said than done. While dads may feel sad when they have to say good-bye to their children, moms normally experience the pain of letting go more intensely, especially with daughters.

As I shared in my book *When Mothers Pray,* releasing our children is perhaps the hardest work of motherhood, and that's why we resist it. Our "monster mother thing," the Mama Bear heart, is like those little creatures in cereal boxes that grow and grow when you put them in water. Our mother heart emerges when we're expecting and causes us to nurture and protect and care for our child. It's also what fuels a mom to lift a heavy car off her child in an accident or a single mother to work three jobs to send her daughter to a good college so she can reach her dreams. That natural protectiveness also motivates us to put a megafilter on our teenager's computer to shield her from online predators.

But along with this mother role come worry, anxiety, and fear—and the struggle to let go of the active mothering role we've had for so long. It doesn't happen overnight. Usually the releasing process happens in stages, much like letting a kite out. A little string was let out when she took her Princess Barbie lunch box and walked into the kindergarten room, more was let out when she went away to summer camp for two weeks, and that kite string went *way out* when she got the car keys and started driving. You've probably already discovered that letting go isn't a one-time event; it continues to be important throughout our daughters' lives and ours.

But when your beloved daughter piles her flip-flops, iPod, high heels, designer jeans, and earthly belongings in her car, flashes you a smile that cost over $3,000, and leaves home to go to college or to move into an apartment of her own, it's a defining moment. Later, a wedding may call for a deeper letting go. But for now, a page is turned, this chapter is over. The structure of your day changes, especially if this is the last child to leave. Many mothers wonder if they are now irrelevant, what their role will be, or if life will ever be as much fun again. Even if the day-to-day interaction with your daughter involved arguments or power struggles, you still miss her!

EQUIPMENT FOR THE LETTING-GO JOURNEY

Just as you need some basic equipment when you go on a hiking trip, you'll need some things to let your daughter go in a healthy and grace-filled way.

First, *a new set of glasses* with which to see her is in order. We tend to see our child in the same way we did when she was young, but now she's an adult. When she comes home for a visit, it's time to see her in a brand-new light—*as she is now* and not as she was at twelve or seventeen. I know women in their forties who say their mothers still see and treat them as if they were children. Nothing rankles them more.

Change is inevitable, so it helps tremendously to have a positive perspective about our daughters' departure. A recent study of more than three hundred moms and dads whose children were leaving home found that parents who *focused on being proud of their child's growing independence coped best.* "They were able to step back from daily parenting tasks and look at their kids as being adults, even peers," says Christine Proulx, assistant professor of human development and family studies at the University of Missouri, where the study was done. Instead of focusing on what you've lost, Proulx suggested to consider what you're gaining: more time for hobbies and relationships.[3]

Next, you'll need *an open heart plus willingness to see your own part in any rift or misunderstanding with your daughter, and the courage to admit it.* We go into this subject more in chapter 13, "The Power of Forgiveness." An open mind may come in handy if your daughter has different political views or lifestyle choices or chooses a boyfriend you'd *never* have chosen for her.

The letting-go process will also be advanced if you are selfless enough to consider her needs instead of being preoccupied with how you're feeling. If she makes mistakes or her life is tumultuous for a while, don't blame yourself. It's easy to take on guilt and compare our daughters to all the women we know who are living stellar lives, but it doesn't help either of you.

Add a large measure of supportiveness, not just tolerance of your daughter's growing independence. For example, Leslie's daughter Mandy went to college to get a degree in social work. After the second year, she came home and said, "I can't stand this field or these people."

Instead of telling her daughter that if she dropped out of college now it would be a failure or a waste of her parents' money, Leslie responded, "It's good you know this now. It's part of discovering who you are and what you want to do." After some discussion with her parents, Mandy told them she wanted to go to California and be a nanny. She'd thought about it for a long time.

"It was hard to let her go," Leslie said, "but that was her choice, and I wanted to support her growing independence. She was twenty-one and had very good reasons to go." Though she had no job set up, Mandy quickly got a nanny job and an apartment and is happy. "She always manages to land on her feet, and it's built a lot of confidence," her mom said. Letting your daughter be herself is part of building a friendship.

Lastly, you'll need *a large dose of faith* to believe that although you love your daughter immensely, God loves her even more. You can trust him to love and care for her even when you aren't around. It reminds me of an old description of faith: "Genuine faith puts its letter in the mailbox and lets go. Distrust, however, holds on to a corner of the envelope and then wonders why the answer never arrives."

I've found by talking to many women that it's easier to let go when everything's going well with our daughters—when they're making choices we approve of and being responsible and honest with us. However, if our daughters are experiencing problems—whether it's an illness, addiction, eating disorders, financial irresponsibility, consequences from poor choices—or if our family is dysfunctional or in crisis, it complicates the letting-go process. Our daughters may leave us physically, but emotionally and mentally we may still hang on—or they do.

Such was our experience.

THE BROKENNESS OF ADDICTION

When our three children were growing up, we were a loving, healthy family for almost twenty years. My husband, Holmes, and I were devoted parents and loved the adventure of life and family. We gave parenting and our children all we had. And the five of us had great fun together. We were not a perfect family but a little flock who loved God and one another—and had the potential to continue being a functional, connected family.

Until a horrible, cunning invader entered our lives when our oldest son was in college, the next was a senior in high school, and Ali was a sophomore. This invader—the disease of alcoholism—was not invited yet wreaked havoc on our family. As in most families this disease invades, it brought patterns of fear, shame, denial, hiding, and secrecy, which hurt our relationships.

A look at the reality of how many families are devastated by this intruder got me out of the illusion that we're alone. According to Sharon Hersh, licensed therapist and author of *The Last Addiction: Why Self-Help Is Not Enough*, "Addiction has left countless individuals and families broken into a million little pieces."[4] It certainly did ours.

She references Robert R. Perkinson's comprehensive report on drug and alcohol addiction released in 2004 that showed "there is not a family in America that has not been impacted by addiction"[5]—whether that's an addiction to substances, gambling, pornography, shopping, or food.

And it's not just the person struggling with addiction whose life is damaged. As Hersh says, "Often family members suffer equally, if not more. The family members' sense of shame highlights the last addiction—the addiction to ourselves—because family and friends of the addict often erroneously believe, "*I* should have done something. *I* should be able to stop this. If *I* just knew what to do, what to say, how to be, the addict would get better."[6] That is exactly what I felt.

Hersh's explanation describes our family to a tee, and her definition of the codependent was on target as well: "the tendency to immerse myself in the lives of people I care about while forgetting to look at myself."[7] Oh, how I immersed myself in taking care of my children and husband and trying to deal with any obstacles to their well-being. To a fault. Alcoholism runs in my family, so to protect my kids from this disease, I became a teetotaler and encouraged Holmes to do the same so they wouldn't grow up around alcohol. Plus I gave them lots of information on the dangers of alcohol and on our family's genetic makeup so they would avoid it. Yet, with all my efforts, my sweet husband from a proper family, despairing of life when his business crashed, started secretly drinking. I felt I'd failed.

Because I wanted to be a good mother, this failure was very hard to face. It was easier to try to improve my husband and blame him when he didn't cooperate, which I did for a long time. I also grew lonely, angry at him, and hurt that God would let this happen…and very, very sad.

One of the characteristics of this disease is the addict's emotional absence. My husband and I loved each other and were loyal and committed, but alcoholism caused disconnectedness and brokenness in our marriage and family. Since Ali adored her dad, she felt emotionally abandoned by him at a crucial time of her life. And she was frustrated at me for staying in what looked like a miserable marriage. It was miserable at certain points, which is not uncommon.

As Sharon Hersh says, when there is addiction in a family, it "immerses you in a world that you would have never chosen. It takes up all the air in the room, leaving you gasping for breath. When you are in a relationship with someone who is struggling with an addiction, you are always scrambling for a solution to the problem and 'waiting for the other shoe to drop' at the same time, which leaves very little energy for self-care."[8] It also means you are distracted from meeting the emotional needs of your child.

I kept living in denial because alcoholism was so terrifying, and my husband kept hiding it because it was so shameful.

Don't get me wrong, when I saw him drink too much at a wedding once or twice a year, I did the good ol' codependent routine—try to get him to stop! Surely another lecture or a really motivating pep talk about all the reasons he shouldn't drink more than two beers at any event would help. I convinced him to go to counseling when we could afford it. Yet while trying to solve this baffling problem, I became more isolated from friends and felt increasingly depressed and guilty that I couldn't solve this problem.

When one person has an addiction, it affects each person in the family in individual and often profound ways. Sadly, this invader not only deepened my husband's chronic depression, it hurt our marriage and his career and wrecked our finances. It also impacted our relationships with our kids and particularly mine with Ali. For many families that have a person struggling with a drinking problem, everyone walks on eggshells, tries to meet his or her needs and makes sure this person is not upset. In the meantime, other family members' needs fall by the wayside, causing resentment, sadness, anger, and low self-esteem. That was especially true of Ali, because she was the youngest. In the midst of the family problems, she had become depressed.

I was concerned about Ali's depression and wanted to "fix her"; she was concerned about my overload and depletion. We worried about each other in codependent, unhealthy ways. She was always giving me advice about how I should fix my life, and I dispensed my share of advice back to her. She felt sorry for me but angry too because she didn't feel she could vent that on her dad, feeling he was too fragile.

Two years ago my husband and I embarked on the lifelong journey of recovery with the gracious help of the Jim Riley Outreach (www.jimrileyoutreach.org) of Edmond, Oklahoma. Ali had begun her own journey of recovery a year before. Our marriage is happier than it's been in years, though we still face uncertainties and challenges. And we love grandparenting together. We do believe and have experienced that when we stay committed to Christ and our spouse, God can put a family back together. I deeply respect the courage it took for both Ali and Holmes to enter recovery. They've inspired me, and I am truly thankful for how far we've come.

We share our story and this book, praying that the One who redeems tragic or seemingly devastating situations will take what we've learned and allow you to use it in a way that would help you understand your daughter, a friend, or family member—if not right now, perhaps in years ahead.

Your family situation may not resemble ours; what brought distance between Ali and me may not be an issue for you. But each family has its own problems, its own dysfunctions that affect relationships. Perhaps with three daughters, one felt you favored the others, and that brought a rift between you. Or your husband left you, and as a single mom you were overloaded and your daughter targeted you to receive her angry feelings. You were the safe place to vent. If one of your kids had a chronic, serious illness that took most of your attention, or if your daughter made choices that catapulted her life into destruction during the teen years, it can bring distance or tension in the mother-daughter relationship. Maybe something else has resulted in a lack of closeness you wish you had with your adult daughter. Whatever the causes, you can rebuild your relationship; you can reconnect in new ways.

DESPERATE TO DO SOMETHING

When Ali graduated from high school, I *thought* I was releasing her. Saying good-bye as my child packed up to leave wasn't a new experience; I'd already done it twice when our sons went to college. When she lived in another city for two years doing youth work and began to experience tough times, she'd occasionally call me and share a problem. I became burdened for her and poured out my heart to God and filled my journal with prayers for Ali. I gave her back to God again countless times and prayed some more…and some more. But nothing seemed to change.

One day when she called sounding very depressed, a friend and I got in my car to take her to lunch. We're *not* talking about picking her up across town for a quick bite—but driving *four hundred miles* to take my daughter to a restaurant. Perhaps that demonstrates the degree of concern and codependency. I wanted to rescue her out of her pain, to see if there was anything I could do to help and be a support.

I operated in a solution-oriented, how-to kind of thinking. I so wanted to fix her and help her be happier. The codependent part of our relationship made me think, *If only Ali gets happy and things go better for her, if she gets going in a positive direction and is less depressed, then not only will she be happier—I'll be happier too.* It was breaking my heart to see her so unhappy, and I wanted to *do something.*

I truly didn't know there was an option to admit that I was powerless over places, things, and people—including my daughter and her circumstances. I didn't know I could find my own happiness in the midst of that season and live my own life. After all, one of my roles in my family of origin and throughout life had been to be perpetually positive (no bad moods allowed), cheer people up, solve problems.

Even with the most loving intentions when I was "just trying to help," my codependent, enmeshed thinking and behavior didn't help anyone. It certainly didn't contribute to Ali's well-being. One of the most valuable discoveries I've made is that if we base our happiness on people, situations, places, or especially *someone we love changing,* then we are putting off our own joy. And we aren't really letting go.

THE GIFT OF LETTING GO

As hard as it may be, we must let go if our daughter is going to have the confidence to be her own person as a complete, equal adult who builds a successful life as who she's created to be. It's a wonderful gift we give her—the gift of independence and acceptance *at whatever stage of life she is in.*

Sometimes it's a daughter who leans too heavily on her mother, wanting Mom to fix every serial, crazy situation. If that's your situation, it's in her best interest to stop bailing your daughter out if she gets in trouble. If she goes to college and ends up with credit card debt, for example, let go of the compulsion to rescue. That sends a powerful—and ultimately more helpful—message that your daughter is grown up, that she can work things out herself. We can support and advise if asked, but we should not solve everything for our daughters.

The reality is, if a mom keeps fixing and rescuing, her daughter has less of a chance to practice solving problems and overcome adversity. If mom doesn't let go, a daughter can't come back on her own free will to *choose connection.* The relationship with her mother will be obligatory. If we don't acknowledge with our words *and* our actions that our daughter is now an adult who can handle life without our interference, then we undermine her growth and set the stage for a tumultuous relationship.

For example, if you meet her fiancé and advise her that he's not good enough, or you manage her finances even though she's working and living in her own apartment, or on a visit to her home you rearrange her kitchen without being asked, it's a good sign you haven't let go.

When we don't let go, our daughters hear *control* in everything we do and say—even if we're "just trying to help." The result is a growing hostility. Letting go is the first step toward repairing the breach and a huge step toward meaningful connection.

SEPARATION WITH CONNECTION

As we've shared, our daughters *need* separation—to leave home and grow up—but no matter what their age, daughters *also need* connection to their moms. They especially need to know we're okay with changes in the relationship and that we're willing to give them space when they need it. In chapter 7, we'll share ways to stay connected and yet not be enmeshed or smothering.

Anna, a friend who is in her thirties, has one of the healthiest and most peaceful relationships I've ever seen between a mother and daughter. Her mom, Tracy, knew she'd miss her when she left home, but she made some choices early on that helped the letting-go process take place as it needed to. Tracy had decided to observe her kids and pick up on cues of when they needed autonomy. Anna wanted autonomy right out of high school. She wanted to work and live on her own and ultimately become an artist.

Anna moved out of state and worked to put herself through college a little bit at a time. She pursued the life of an artist and took some unconventional steps of getting there, including working part time in an after-school art program and setting up her own art shows at friends' businesses. She tried things, and if they didn't work, she would try something different. She worked hard and grew resilient. She was innovative and full of self-assurance because of her mom's confidence in her—not to do everything perfectly but to try new things and pick herself up if she faltered.

Tracy had decided she wouldn't interfere or give advice after her daughter left home unless Anna asked for it. It was her life to live and navigate. Anna considered this to be her mom's greatest strength—letting her daughter be herself. She didn't compare Anna to her sisters or brother, she didn't impose her own wishes on her or live vicariously through her, and she definitely didn't rescue her. She was available for phone calls and would offer her thoughts when asked, but other than that, she let Anna do life knowing her mom believed in her.

As I talked with Tracy, she said that what kept her buoyed about her daughter during those years was learning how to launch out and do new things herself and being grateful for the moments she and Anna had together. The occasional phone chat over coffee, even though they weren't across from each other at a table. Or exchanging e-mails here and there to check in. The more Tracy lowered her expectations of their evolving relationship, the better it became and the more Anna wanted her to interact in her life.

PROCESSING OUR FEELINGS

While it's essential that we let go of our daughters, no one ever said it would be easy. Since they were born, we've been highly involved in their lives—from diaper changing and feeding to first steps and first dance classes, throughout school, sports, friends, curfews, and everything in between. We've spent years watching out for them. We've loved nurturing and caring for their needs, praying for them, providing for them, and often dispensing *lots of advice* and instruction about everything from homework to appropriate clothing to proper nutrition.

Even as we're excited about her senior prom and graduation, we know it's coming: that bittersweet experience when a daughter leaves home. It's a loss we need to grieve, so it's normal and appropriate that we should feel sad. Not that we don't have anything to do after our daughter leaves. Our job, volunteer commitments, relationship with a husband if we have one may keep us busy. Maybe it's that we miss her presence at the dinner table every night, shopping together, or late-night chats. We might even miss her loud music and messy room!

Stuffing or denying all those emotions isn't helpful. Instead, it's important to be honest and share them with a trusted girlfriend or spouse. *Don't dump those emotions on your daughter;* it will only make her feel guilty about leaving, and she doesn't need that on her first flight out of the nest or any other time. We can say we miss her and at the same time validate the excitement she feels at being on her own. When we acknowledge our feelings, we get over our sadness sooner and are more likely to adjust to the transition instead of descending into depression.

Having sad or lonely feelings is entirely normal when a child leaves home. A mother may feel listless or a little blue. She may drag around and be unmotivated the first few weeks, or cry or feel nostalgic as she looks in her daughter's room. The house feels too quiet and empty without her laughter and friends around. Even though it's normal, most moms grieve when a child moves out because we know we can't go back and relive the fun and feel the pride.

When a daughter leaves, some moms begin to regret their shortcomings and realize that now there are no do-overs. If this is the case, the best thing we can do for our daughters and our relationships is to talk about it and not wallow in the guilt. If we don't, it's easy to become an overfunctioning mother, and later, grandmother, as we try to make up for lost time. Instead, we can acknowledge our misplaced priorities and release ourselves from guilt so that we can intentionally enjoy the moments we do have with our daughters in the present.

If sadness doesn't diminish as the weeks go by or you have difficulty with "getting a life" apart from your child, then it's time to get some professional help from a licensed counselor. One thing we've heard over and over is that when daughters leave, whether for college, marriage, or a job across the country, they want to know their moms are okay and are taking care of themselves so they don't have to worry about them. Self-care is a gift you give yourself *and your daughter,* and we'll look at ways to do that in chapter 12.

Keep in mind that your daughter will be back. Perhaps she'll return at holiday time or for summer vacation, even though that "coming home" will have challenges all its own. And don't forget, if grandchildren come along down the road, your house will again be filled with the laughter and mess that kids generate.

LETTING GO

Practically speaking, here's what letting go looks like:

To let go doesn't mean to stop caring.

To let go isn't to enable but allow your daughter to learn from natural consequences.

To let go means to admit powerlessness and realize the outcome isn't in my hands.

To let go is not to fix but be supportive.

To let go isn't to protect your daughter from reality but allow her to face it.

To let go is not to nag, scold, or argue but discover your own shortcomings and correct them.[9]

SEEING HER POINT OF VIEW

It sometimes helps to see this transition and new season of your daughter's life from *her point of view.* To do this, think back to how you felt when the doors flew open and you left for the university for your freshman year or for a job in another city. During the first few weeks, were you excited? happy? nervous? confident? homesick?

Maybe you felt a little like I did when my parents dropped me and my stuff at the dorm at Baylor University an hour and a half south of Dallas: *Hooray! I'm going to be on my own! I'm starting college!* I'd always loved school, so I was enthusiastic about this new academic challenge. I'd looked forward to being on campus for months. I couldn't wait to find the suite my roommates and I were sharing and decorate it with our matching Kmart orange corduroy bedspreads and set up the stereo.

Maybe instead of college, you set out to be a flight attendant or missionary, or you moved to another city and went to work. *How did you feel* when you embarked on your adventures out of the nest? Then think about how your daughter might feel. This is wonderful fodder for discussions with your friends who have also said farewell to a child.

A Daughter's Perspective

Part of being a daughter is the desire to be let go. Increasingly through the years, I've wanted my mom to trust me and believe that I am a grown woman now, capable of making my own decisions and living life well.

As a daughter, being let go feels like healthy freedom. It feels like we're free to be who we were created to be without needing to explain or apologize to our mothers. When you let us go, it helps us know you're going to be okay and have a life outside of us. It tells us you trust us to use the tools you gave us. It gives us a sense that we can leave your house and come back on occasion—mistakes and all—for a hug or hot meal and then go out again like we're supposed to because we're adults.

Since I was the third child, my brothers had already broken my mom in for the whole leaving/letting-go drill. So in some ways, I found that it was startlingly easy for my mom to see me graduate and leave that first year. Later on I realized what was hardest for her was to know I was unhappy. I endured a breakup, financial troubles, and other typical twenty-something maladjusted behaviors. What I wanted most from my mom was to get a pep talk and then a big confidence booster like: "Nothing can bring you down; you can do this; you can get through this; you're a strong woman…"

Instead, I felt that I was causing so much worry by my instability and mood swings that I began shutting down. Ultimately, the one person I wanted to confide in was the one person I deliberately shut out. I sensed that my unhappiness too easily became hers; it felt awful to know that my choices, moods, and experiences had such a profound effect on my mom. I knew she had her own major stressors, so I decided to keep mine from her. Thus, our pattern of relating got more and more out of sync.

While Mom let me go physically, with grace and seeming ease, emotionally she couldn't let go. I sensed her worry through her language, facial expressions, her mention of "Ali and prayer" in the same sentence a few times a day. I felt that I needed to be happy and conversational around my mother. Something in me said, "No! I want my bad moods if I want them. I want that angst if I want it! Give me my pain!"

You could say I was having twenty-something toddler moments. The angst of life was my comfort blanket, and I didn't want to give it up. I didn't want my mom to try to cheer me up or worry about me. Deep down what I really needed and wanted was for Mom to be okay with my sadness. Believe me, I'm not proud to admit this stuff, but it helps to be aware that we all go through chemically, hormonally, out-of-whack times. If any of this gives you insight into your own daughter's ill or dark moods, then it wasn't all for naught.

Plus, now I know that this sometimes crazy pattern of relating actually has a name: codependency. I'm defining codependency as not being able to let go of someone emotionally, spiritually, or physically.

It's difficult. I get that now; I'm beginning the process with my own kids. But I'm choosing to let go even when it's hard and stings—those heart pangs—because I know that releasing leads to peace. And the more peace, the more the relationship can air out and grow. We daughters need and want to know you can let go of us without your life falling apart, without causing a huge upheaval. We want to know it's okay to go live our adult lives and to feel your blessing for the distance. As my mom has let go more and more, she's learned to trust and believe that I'm a capable adult who is launching out in new adventures with the good foundation she and my dad gave me. This feels so freeing and has instilled confidence in me, especially as it relates to my parenting. Every time she's stepped back and let me do my own thing, the way I want to do it, my respect for her grows immensely, and I want to include her more in the "figuring-out process" in my various stages of life.

Since going back to school recently, I've sought more advice and input from my mom because we've grown less and less codependent in the past two years. When I wonder how I'm going to keep juggling college, kids, and work and stay sane, she responds with an air of confidence in me that I might not have at that stressful moment. She says something like, "Oh, it's just a busy phase, but it's exciting and I know you can do it. Do you want me to watch the boys tonight so you can study?" She's practical and empowering when I have my "moody moments."

Because she learned to let go, my mom's peace of mind concerning my choices and ups and downs no longer changes. We just have new ways of dealing with the stress—like movie night and other fun ways to connect, which we'll talk more about later on.

Two-Part Harmony

There are benefits and blessings to embracing the new seasons of our daughters' lives—for both them and for us moms.

What if your daughter's out-of-the-nest years are stormy or she criticizes everything you do? Once I (Cheri) talked with a wise counselor who raised four children into adulthood and counseled hundreds of families throughout her career. She told me that mothers often came to her tearfully describing how mean their teenage son or daughter treats them, how they curse at her and are disrespectful.

"What have I done to deserve this? What have I done wrong?" they ask her. She tells them that this behavior shows how close that child feels to mom. So close in fact that to separate enough to stand on their own two feet, they have to push her away because part of them really wants to curl up in her lap as they did when they were younger. Though that explanation doesn't take away the hurt you may feel if your daughter separated in a negative, rebellious way, we hope it helps bring some understanding and comfort about the process that's going on.

If your daughter's life is a mess right now, see her life as an unfinished work that God can handle. During certain phases of your daughter's life, she may need some distance from you. That's okay. Detaching, letting go, can give you those new glasses with which to see the real woman she is becoming. As your "eyesight" gets better, your heart will grow, and you'll see new characteristics, perhaps surprising changes and healthy growth.

Regardless of how difficult the process, the upside of letting go is how it enables you to change your view of your daughter and to allow a mutually satisfying friendship to develop between you. Another benefit is when she leaves the nest, you'll also have time to pursue dreams you once put aside. As you are willing to loosen the reins, your daughter will be that much freer to become herself *and* come back to you, woman to woman, with respect and appreciation for letting her go—which ultimately builds a strong and satisfying bond for both of you.

GENERATIONAL DIFFERENCES

- - - - -

Grant us the serenity to avoid using checks with seagulls on them, the courage to bypass poodle-shaped oven mitts, and the wisdom to know the difference between our mothers and ourselves.
—SUZANNE FINNAMORE, *O, THE OPRAH MAGAZINE*

- - - - -

very generation is different from the generation before, yet we also share some similarities. Sometimes the conflict or distance between mothers and daughters is about our not understanding each other's generation. That's why in this chapter we are going to cover two aspects of generational issues that affect that relationship: first, the vast differences between our daughters' generation and ours, and second, the cycle of hurt or negative patterns passed on to us from our mothers, which we often pass along to our daughters.

You see, the mother-daughter relationship isn't a narrow one defined only by a mom and her daughter, but also by two generations in the here and now. The complexities—which are sometimes wounds passed down, a critical spirit, or other patterns of behavior—that affect both mother and daughter are a tapestry woven with mothers and daughters from generations and generations back. As you'll see in the pages ahead, sometimes these hinder our journey to reconcile and understand each other in the present.

A DIFFERENT WORLD, A DIFFERENT GENERATION

As we worked on this project, over and over we heard things from women such as:

- "My mother doesn't value my lifestyle because I haven't married right out of college and had children. In fact, I didn't finish college but went to culinary school. I have a great career and a life I'm happy with, but she doesn't approve."
- "My mother doesn't get it; she thinks my tattoo is a moral problem when it's no big deal. It's just a tattoo."
- "I send almost two hundred text messages a day and receive about that many. That's just the way my friends and I communicate. If my mom would start texting, we could keep in better touch."
- "I don't want to get tied down to a husband, kids, and a pressure-filled work schedule early on like my mom did, but she doesn't understand that. By my age she had three kids. I got a job teaching on a military base in Germany so I could travel and have no plans to settle down."

Our daughters grew up in a different world than we did.

Here are some comments daughters made about the contrast between their moms' generation and theirs:

- "I think women are listened to and respected today more than in my mom's generation…the whole doormat-wife thing. Also there is more freedom and choice for women today to have a career and be single. It isn't looked down on. Education offers more options for us."

- "'Don't talk' and 'husband is master' was the perspective of my mother's generation. That's not the way we women see it today."

- "I think one difference is the perception of opportunity. I have always felt that all opportunities were open to me and sense that my mother's generation was constricted and had fewer open opportunities because of their gender. I never felt constricted in education, sports, dating, career, etc., because of being female."

- "Another difference might be the perceived pressure to *do it all*—the career, the 'wifing,' the professionalism, the parenting, the making a difference. If all options are open to us, having to choose which ones to pursue can be challenging. Must we have to quit one in order to pursue the other? I chose to go back to work on a flex-schedule when my baby was six weeks old, and Mom thought I should stay home."

- "Technology is a major difference between our mothers' and our generation. Social networking is an integral part of our lives, both at work and home: blogs, texts, twittering, Facebook, and whatever the new means of electronic communication is."

UNDERSTANDING OUR DAUGHTER'S GENERATION

According to researcher Rosalind C. Barnett, the enormous differences between their lives and generations is a major source of conflict and misunderstanding between mothers and daughters today. "Among the areas of greatest difference are education, career, birth control, divorce. Compared to our mothers, we are considerably better educated, are engaged in a wider range of career options and activities, are able to shape our reproductive lives both in terms of the number and timing of our children, and are much freer to end destructive marriages"[1]—and to live together but not marry. In addition, more than five million unmarried couples cohabit in the U.S., nearly eight times the number in 1970, and a record-breaking 40 percent of babies born in 2007 had unmarried parents—that's up 25 percent from 2002.[2]

Women from college age through their forties are the first generation of women to grow up knowing *all doors* are open for them: CEO of a major corporation, transplant surgeon, secretary of state, Speaker of the House, or president of the United States.

Many women today carve out their own paths. With so many opportunities, they may be anxious or overburdened by the many hats they wear and the high expectations their parents put on them to succeed. Yet they take on challenges in spite of the stress.

Daughters tend to feel much less pressure to marry than their mothers did, often marry later, and delay having children. If they are in a marriage that's unhappy or toxic, they are more likely to divorce.[3] They feel little compulsion to submit and stay. The differences in reproductive rights and access to birth control are vast as well. And yes, technology has changed the lifestyles of these texting, iPhone- and iPod-using women. They've grown up with computers and electronics and usually have far more expertise at using them than their moms do.

It's easy to be critical of the differences. A sixty-something woman I talked to recently told me, "My daughter's generation (thirties) doesn't know how to communicate face to face because they're always texting. They're not as hard working as my generation was either, and they don't face reality very well." She went on to criticize their tendency to self-medicate and be dreamers.

But the truth is, though some of her opinions may be valid, every generation has strengths and weaknesses. So we have a choice: we can be negative and focus on the younger generation's weaknesses, or we can look for the strengths and believe that their generation is going to produce more outstanding world leaders or be even better parents than we've been. When we make the choice to *believe in their generation,* we empower our daughters and can call into action the best in them.

Doing the opposite—being critical—is discouraging, as a young woman expressed, "My mom says my generation takes things for granted and we're lazy. It's so defeating to hear those negative things; it makes me want to fall into that stereotype since that's what she believes about us."

CELEBRATING THE DIFFERENCES

I love some things about women in their twenties, thirties, and forties, such as their ability to talk about their dilemmas and issues with honesty, sometimes a raw honesty that makes their moms uncomfortable. Their lack of pretense and focus on appearances is refreshing, and they have a clearer sense of boundaries than we did. Many of them make it a priority to stay closely connected with their girlfriends, having regular girls' nights out at a restaurant or an overnight getaway.

Yet with all the differences, I see our commonality: just like us, women today are looking for connections in every season of life, including one with their moms. If we can focus on how we are alike and avoid wanting our daughters to be just like us or our generation of women, we can forge an even better relationship.

A great place to start is to be intentional in appreciating the good things about your daughter's generation. Think of something specific. Do your daughter and her friends reach out to women in a shelter or people in Africa through humanitarian projects, donate money to charities via the Internet, or care about protecting the environment? Is going green and doing environmentally friendly things like recycling and driving a hybrid car important to her? When you affirm those qualities, it boosts your daughter's sense of value, which enhances your relationship. Consider other strengths and find a time when you could acknowledge them.

A Daughter's Perspective

I agree with Mom that understanding the unique characteristics of your daughter's generation can help immensely in relating to her. As she has shared, we are coming from a different time and culture and thus are definitely unique, but we too want to connect with you, our moms!

As you begin to realize aspects of our generation—in light of your own and your mother's—you'll be better able to relate to your daughter. If she's like my friends and me, she wants you to understand that *it's not about you* if she rejects your style or way of doing things, for example, if she becomes a mom but also has a career (and you think she ought to stay home), or if she chooses to be a stay-at-home mom when you thought she'd be a corporate exec.

We daughters want you moms to know that we feel misunderstood and rejected when you reject our style or ways of doing things based on generational differences. It feels like criticism of the here and now and how we operate in the present era. Please know that we value you and where you've come from. We admire the way you've adapted to all the changes that you have. And we want to feel equally valued and applauded for our adaptability to the culture we live in.

We might choose to wait until we feel settled financially and career-wise before we invest in a serious relationship, and we want you to understand that we've thought a lot about our decision. We grew up with the divorce rate at 50 percent and still climbing. We've seen flaws in the more traditional ways of approaching things, and maybe we are trying something new and different because we don't want to end up a statistic. We might believe there's life outside the white picket fence and trying to find our happiness in a mate. Even so, we want more of the same things than you think, just in a different order or timing.

We're less likely to feel limited in the workplace because of being female than you were, and we probably don't feel like anything, anyone, or any cultural ideal is keeping us from achieving the goals we want to achieve. We may choose to get into politics or to be a pastor or to give our talents and time to something outside the home. If or when we have children, we may likely still choose to work outside the home and contribute to the world financially, politically, musically, intellectually, and inspirationally.

We want you to celebrate with us our unique opportunity in this quickly changing world. Maybe the very thing you are bemoaning (like a new cell phone or computerized gadget) could be a bonding experience instead of a point of contention. Your adult daughter (who may be far more competent than you realize) would probably love to help you learn something that might even make your life easier. If you showed some interest in her latest gadget, you could both end up benefiting and bonding from simply being open to something outside your comfort zone.

That's the case in Stella's and Sophie's connection with their mom. Stella goes to community college, Sophie works two jobs and is getting married in September. They all keep in touch through sending tons of text messages each week, and they think their mother is cool to enter into the social networking they're into. Fortunately, they have an unlimited plan with their cell phones.

By accepting (not necessarily agreeing with) your daughter's generation, you build a hugely important bridge that gives you greater access into your daughter's world in general.

AM I BECOMING MY MOTHER?

We've been talking about our daughters in this book, but it's also important to reflect on what our experience was like when we were daughters ourselves, and what parenting behaviors our mothers passed down to us.

The complexities that affect both mother and daughter are a tapestry woven with mothers and daughters from generations and generations back. They are ghosts of the past that haunt us in our journey to try to reconcile with each other and are sometimes only found through counseling or getting honest with a trusted friend.

Most of our moms passed down many important values: a strong work ethic or faith, resourcefulness, loyalty to family, or a deep sense of commitment. I know mine did, and I am deeply grateful also for Mama's example of hospitality and home-making, her optimism and earnest prayers for all the family, her caring for those less fortunate—she bought brand-new shoes for children in a local orphanage every Easter, for example.

But sometimes mothers pass on negative qualities, such as a critical spirit, a hair-trigger temper, or a controlling, dominant temperament. If yours did, you're not alone.

"Maybe your mother was flawless, but it's more likely she made mistakes," says Martha Beck. "Perhaps she was occasionally impatient, unappreciative of the creativity you displayed… Maybe she was distracted by other concerns: finances, illness, alcoholism… Whatever her errors, to the extent that your mother was not perfect, you inherited a legacy of sorrow."[4] And the ways they mothered us affects our mothering. This was certainly the case for me and many of the women I interviewed.

My mother and many other women in her generation lived through the Great Depression and World War II. Her family was poor, since her father, a carpenter, was unemployed during her growing-up years. Much of the time her mother traveled with Mama's older twin sisters, who were professional dancers, and sent money home for basic necessities — so she didn't grow up with a mother's nurture and care. Though she was valedictorian of her large high school class in Houston, Texas, there was no money for college, so she had to go to work full time. She had worked part time and weekends throughout high school, so she made a lateral move from the downtown Kress department store to being ticket-girl at the movie theater.

Mama's work ethic was off the charts. She hated messy houses. Having endured a chaotic home because she grew up mostly with her father's and brothers' messiness and addictions, order was vital to her sense of well-being. With six children, it took a lot of work to keep everything neat and in order. Dads went to their jobs and did not help with housework in those days. She sewed most of our clothes and made sure she never went to bed at night until all the little dresses, every towel, cloth diaper, and item of clothing was washed, dried, folded, and put away. That goes for washing dishes and having a clean house as well.

Cooking three meals a day on a shoestring for a family of eight plus grandparent or neighbor drop-ins was a load, but Mama never complained. We were enlisted to do dishes and make beds when we were old enough, but I could rarely make my bed as well as Mama wanted it done.

"Cleanliness is next to godliness" was her watchword, and she lived by it, not only with her home but improving every place she went (like dusting the interior of a plane with her linen handkerchief when she got on and off).

I remember watching her cook or sweep, and cook or sweep some more, throughout the day and evening, *longing* for her to sit down and just talk to me. But usually she was too busy. It was *not* the cultural norm to have "special time" with your kids in those days. When adults gathered, the "children should be seen and not heard" philosophy reigned, and my two younger siblings and I ate in the kitchen if there were guests. Mom was a devoted homemaker and enormously hospitable.

Yet somewhere in the back of my mind I was probably thinking, *All Mama does is pick up, pick up, and pick up. I won't be like that when I have kids!*

Years later, after I had children of my own, a college student named Amy lived in our two-story home one summer. Whenever I went upstairs, I took stuff with me that was sitting on the staircase and put it away in the bedrooms and then brought items down on the way. One afternoon as Amy was standing in the upstairs hall talking to me, I picked up a small load of clothes to take downstairs to the laundry room, having just put Alison's dolls on her bed that I brought from downstairs when I heard Amy say, "Cheri, all you do is pick up and pick up and pick up!"

I had to admit Amy was right. I *did* do a lot of picking up—which I discovered moms do out of necessity. I also had a husband who, like my mother, wanted everything to be tidy, clean, and in order. Still, having fun with my kids and spending time with them was definitely a high priority to me.

Sue, a woman I know, told me her mom was a hard-working Michigan farm wife. There were two kids, and her mother had tasks to do from morning till night. There was no sitting down for chitchat! Though she did volunteer at her children's school occasionally, Sue doesn't remember a time that she and her mom just went out for lunch in town together or sat at the kitchen table to share thoughts over a cup of tea. She couldn't really ask her mother questions—it was just *not done*.

When Sue became a mother herself, she was determined to be different from her mother. She was a far more relational mother with her two children, who are now in their twenties. While she was expected to ride the big yellow school bus that picked up the farm kids, Sue drove her son and daughter to school and sports, just to have the opportunities to communicate with them in the car. Her daughter knew she could ask her mom about *everything,* and she did. Sue made time for her children and got on their "turf," even watching the weekly *America's Next Top Model* show with her daughter though she wasn't interested in it.

"My mom wouldn't have done that; she didn't have time for TV or movies," Sue related to me. She truly respected her mother, but they never were adult friends.

In their twenties, Sue's son and daughter are closer to their mom than she was to hers. They keep in touch during the day via text and instant messaging (she got on their "electronic turf" also), and Sue and her daughter enjoy going to live musical theater or shopping for antiques.

FROM MOTHER TO DAUGHTER TO GRANDDAUGHTER

Here's a story that illustrates how this "passing on from mom to daughter to granddaughter" principle works and what effect it can have on your relationship. Because you see, Ali and my mother-daughter "duet" began not just with us but first with my petite, five-foot-three mom.

One summer weekend between semesters of college, I was to drive my mom down to Galveston, Texas, from Dallas to meet her husband (my stepfather). I had just arrived home from my freshman year and invited my friend Ann to ride along with us. However, as we threw our bags in the trunk, my mother said, "No, I don't want you to drive, Cheri! You'd scare me too much. Ann, you get in the front seat and drive."

Mama probably didn't realize it, but I was humiliated in front of my friend and stung by the lack of confidence she had, not only in my driving but in *me.* She had what the family called "car anxiety" and did a lot of backseat driving, including using her invisible brake. Although I asked her to reconsider and told her I was able to drive us safely to the coast, she wouldn't hear of it. She thought my friend would do a better job. I was living on my own on the university campus most of the year, yet Mama was still *quite in charge.* A wad of frustration and hurt sunk deep within and remained there all the way down I-35.

Sitting in the front passenger seat, Mama chatted cheerily with my friend. At one point she asked, "Why are you so quiet, Cheri?" I was doing a slow burn in the backseat, mentally defending myself. *I've been driving for several years, never had a ticket. I'm a good driver, and I've driven her lots of places.* Yet there was no room to talk about the issue or tell Mama how I felt about it. What she said went, and that was it. Taking that trip with her didn't boost my confidence, nor did it help our relationship.

Until I talked over this incident with Ali recently, I hadn't realized how the cycle of hurt continued and how I had done a similar thing to her—not once, but a number of times. You see, I was nervous sometimes when my child was driving, just as my mom was. Along with inheriting her blue eyes, I got mom's car anxiety, and a depth perception problem added to that made it seem like the curb or car in front was a lot closer than it seemed to the driver, so I preferred to drive rather than let Ali take the wheel.

YOU KNOW YOU'RE BECOMING YOUR MOTHER WHEN...

- You begin to hum "Over the Rainbow" or your mom's favorite big band song.
- You take a bite of your daughter's food while you're eating at a restaurant at the same moment you say, "You don't mind if I try this, do you?"

- You hand a magazine article to your husband
  or daughter and say, "Read this; you'll learn
  something."
- You pick the lint or long hair off your daughter's
  shoulder and say, "I'm just trying to help."
- You begin making the same faces to your
  daughter your mom made—the "look" when
  she's angry, the cheery face you saw in the
  morning when you wanted to sleep and she
  said, "Rise and shine! This is the day the Lord
  has made!"
- You say things like, "Oh don't worry about me,
  I'm fine; you young people enjoy yourselves."
- You hear yourself telling the ever-famous
  "I remember when..." stories for the second
  or fourth time.

A Daughter's Perspective

When I turned sixteen I was invincible—as most sixteen-year-olds think they are. Driving represented the ultimate freedom. My brothers had attained it long ago it seemed, so when it was my turn it was a long-awaited freedom. I loved driving for the feel of adventure and autonomy it gave me and felt I was really good at it. It was strange; I didn't have a lot of confidence in other areas, but my driving was something special, I believed. Deep down it was something I wanted my mom to appreciate.

Whenever I really wanted to drive if we were going somewhere together and she said "No, I'll drive," I felt like she didn't trust me behind the wheel or she couldn't control the car and so therefore she was closed to the idea. Silly as it sounds now, this still hurts at times. I feel like I'm a child and she's not quite ready still to trust me behind the wheel. I know for a fact that she's come leaps and bounds; we switch off driving when we go down to Dallas together. I drive sometimes when we go to a movie or shopping—and she's a lot more relaxed than she used to be.

So I'd encourage you, moms, if you don't force yourself to get out of the driver's seat and let your daughter drive once in a while, she'll feel like you have trouble trusting in her or believing in her in other areas. I'm glad my mom told me she was sorry she responded out of fear, and you can have that kind of conversation with your daughter too—whether it's about this issue or another.

Two-Part Harmony

Perhaps you see your daughter making the same mistakes you made regarding your life, your husband, or children—and you feel critical and upset. When that happens, it may be because you haven't become aware of how you have passed on your own hurts to your daughter. It may be because there are issues between you and your mom that need forgiveness and healing.

Even if our moms have passed away, we can still feel unforgiveness, misunderstanding, and judgment toward them. And if there's one thing that will keep our relationship with our daughters from getting better, it is not forgiving our own mothers. Often the things that most irritated or wounded us as daughters are the very things we do to our own daughters. This is simply human nature. If we were constantly criticized and under scrutiny by our mothers for our physical appearance or personality, and felt the pain and hurt of the inability to please, and if we held on to that deep hurt, then it's likely that we will continue the cycle of hurt and be critical of someone else—most likely our daughters.

Talking with Ali, I realized that even though my mother's in heaven, I needed to forgive her for what was hurtful to me and to sincerely apologize to Ali for doing some of the same painful things to her. Suffice it to say, it was a very sweet and reconciling moment between us. Now when we get in the car together, we share the driving equally.

Unless we forgive our mothers and recognize the deep wounds within us that need tending to, we pass those hurts along. Then it becomes the job of the next generation to realize, forgive, and change the cycle of hurt. But sometimes the cycle doesn't break, and the circle of hurt and critical words continues.

Wouldn't it be marvelous if we could find a way to heal our own pain and hurt from our mothers and to forgive them? Then we would be motivated to pass along *healing* instead of hurt to our daughters. The bottom line is we love them so much. The bottom line is we want a reunion of our hearts, not power struggles that dogged us in the past, to take precedence in our present relationship.

Someone once said, "Generation after generation of women have pledged to raise their daughters differently, only to find that their daughters grow up and fervently pledge the same thing." We've described some of the differences in our generation and our daughters' and encouraged you to reflect on how your mother's parenting may have negatively affected your own so that you can better accept your daughter, overcome negative patterns of relating, and connect better with who she really is. As I have discovered, our past can be redeemed, and when it is, our daughters are the beneficiaries.

VALIDATING YOUR DAUGHTER

● ● ● ● ●

Hair brings one's self-image into focus; it is vanity's
proving ground. Hair is terribly personal, a tangle of
mysterious prejudices.
—SHANA ALEXANDER

● ● ● ● ●

Hair, makeup, weight, body art—appearance issues cause more tension between mothers and daughters than almost anything else. Sometimes we moms compare and other times we criticize, but neither builds up our daughter or our relationship. In five years of research on mothers and daughters, Deborah Tannen, professor of linguistics at Georgetown University, found that one of the top complaints women have about their moms is that they criticize their looks.[1] Our critique might be couched in a sweet suggestion or question meant to help improve our daughter's appearance, such as, "I thought you were going on a diet" or "What happened to your pretty hair? I liked it the other way."

Even if our intentions are good, our words can still hurt. Criticism and unwanted advice about weight, hair, or appearance undermines our daughter's confidence and can cause her to become irritated and angry with us. Besides reflecting an attempt to control the external aspects of our daughter's life, negative comments leave her feeling unaccepted and thus rejected; they create distance rather than build connection.

Tannen, author of *You're Wearing That?* postulates that when a mother zeroes in on her daughter's appearance, no matter what age she is, she's "regarding her daughter in the same way that she looks at herself in a mirror.… This seemed to account for some of the best and worst aspects of the mother-daughter relationship: Each tends to see the other as a reflection of herself."[2] So it helps to ask ourselves, what do we see when we look in the mirror? Do we like what we see? The more we as mothers are dissatisfied with the internal and external women we are, the more we tend to criticize our daughters. Are we seeing our daughters as a reflection of ourselves? And are we projecting our own self-image on them?

We often do this through comparison—even without realizing it. One day in the counselor's office, Ali and I were discussing how women tend to compare themselves to each other. All of a sudden she said, "Well, Mom, you did that very thing. You thought you were plain compared to your sisters, and I sensed it when we all got together. I took that to mean I was too."

My jaw dropped. I had no idea she was aware of this tendency, nor had I seen how it affected her. Growing up in a houseful of beautiful sisters, I had accepted as some sort of fact that I was plainer than my older sisters, with their dark hair and striking eyes, and my adorable younger sister, as well.

The "I'm plain" impression was once reinforced by a family member (with my boyfriend present) where she commented offhandedly, "Cheri, it's a good thing you're such an achiever, since you're plain." She said later she didn't mean anything negative, but I was mortified.

With dishwater-blond hair, I was told that I looked so different than the other siblings because I was left on the porch by the milkman. They were only kidding, but it didn't boost my self-image. All three older sisters matured early, won beauty contests, and turned heads when they walked into a room. My younger sister won her own crowns too. So I naturally considered my sisters the beautiful ones—they looked more like Mama, who was a real beauty as well, with dark hair, blue eyes, and porcelain skin. Mama never said that one daughter was prettier than the others; it was just the family dynamics of sisters, sibling rivalry, and beauty queens.

I had no idea how comparing myself to my sisters would impact my daughter, or that, as we talked about in the previous chapter, I was inadvertently passing on the same pattern. Holmes and I had been intentional about affirming our sons' and daughter's looks and talents. And as all moms do, I thought our lovely daughter was darling. So it was puzzling why she didn't feel pretty.

Much later I realized that from hearing my "plain" story, Ali interpreted that she was plain too—simply because she's my daughter. Though I'm at peace now with who I am, I realized my insecurities affected my daughter's view of herself. Without knowing it, I had projected my own self-image on her.

If as mothers we're willing to look at our own insecurities or hang-ups regarding our physical appearance—and be open to change—our daughters will respect us for discussing the issue honestly. As hard as it is to face our mistakes, the truth is liberating. Rather than wallowing in regret about this flawed thinking, I told Ali how sorry I was to have passed on that negativity, and it's now become a common ground for us to encourage each other to be our unique selves and be grateful for how we're made—imperfections and all!

We moms don't realize that our daughters feel a certain oneness with us, so if we compare ourselves to others, have hang-ups about our appearance and talk negatively about ourselves, we unknowingly teach our daughters to do the same. They pick up low self-esteem, self-deprecating attitudes, or feelings of being too fat, even when they're a size 6. If we talk about how we've got to lose weight and don't like our size, they tend to become dissatisfied with their own bodies no matter what they look like. All of this is compounded when we're not careful with our "helpful" critiques of how they look.

CRITIQUING THROUGH THE ADULT YEARS

We love our daughters dearly, so why do we criticize them for the way they look? One reason mothers give is wanting them to look their best; another is that this is what our mothers did to us. Some women esteem themselves according to what their daughters look like, or their critique is motivated by a desire for their daughters to look like they do. In addition, if a mother doesn't have love and fulfillment in her life, she may try to fill the emptiness with making her daughter a continual improvement project.

Are we frustrated about our own inability to get to the size we want so we worry about our daughter being overweight? Are we worried about getting older? It helps to remember what Harriet Lerner, PhD, and author of *The Mother Dance,* said, "Everything that is unresolved and stressful in your past and current life will prime you to worry more intensely"[3] about your daughter. I've found from personal experience that those unresolved things from our past also can be transferred to our daughters.

While we often feel it's our job to monitor a daughter's appearance when she is a child or teenager, criticism often continues and may remain a source of irritation in adulthood, even if she becomes a gorgeous movie star or successful businesswoman. Though international model and actress Eva Mendes is stunning on the red carpet, her mom always comments on her daughter's appearance afterward and not always favorably. She'll tell Eva her hair was a bit too elaborate or her heels too high. Eva is one of those rare daughters who is mature and confident enough to take the critique in stride. Despite the negative undertones, she knows her mom is very proud of her and just wants her to shine.

However, most daughters are not this self-assured.

Jen, a married mother of two, was eight months pregnant and had gained the normal amount of weight. When her mom picked her up to go to a great new restaurant one day, she said, "Jen, your cheeks look so puffy." Her scrutiny only made Jen feel more self-conscious than she already was. Her mom couldn't figure out why Jen was silent and apparently irritated at her throughout their lunch.

Somehow mothers feel the freedom to say things to their daughters that other people simply wouldn't say. This is particularly true of straightforward, blunt women. "My daughter and I have open communication and say whatever we feel," said Dorothy. "If I think her hair is too long or she needs to pluck her eyebrows, I tell her. If she's put on a few pounds, I suggest she go to Weight Watchers. She does the same thing to me. It's my job as a mom to give her input, and I welcome hers as well."

While it's nice that this mother isn't rebuffed for her blunt assessment of her thirty-eight-year-old daughter, most adult daughters don't see it as their mother's job to improve the way they look.

A DIFFERENT APPROACH

Suzanne Eller, a youth specialist and author of *The Woman I Am Becoming,* knew her daughters would face enormous pressure in college to fit into a certain mold. She wanted more than ever to let them know that they were women of substance, beautiful inside and out. But she realized she also had to watch what she said about herself. "Did I focus on my own body more than I should? Or did I really *live* what I was saying to my girls?"

She purposed *not* to be critical of their appearance or her own, especially when the girls were in college and consumed with studies and life.

Instead, she asked about what courses they were passionate about and what their plans and dreams were. When they had lunch together, Suzanne didn't focus the conversation on her new exercise program or what her daughters were wearing. Instead, she shared about her new book project and showed interest in the mission trip they were going on during spring break.

"It's a subtle thing that women do to each other," Eller said, "and when all women hear is what they *should look like and should be,* we are undermining their self-worth."[4] Instead, we can be a safe place and validate our daughter's uniqueness, no matter her size, shape, or style. There's nothing more supportive and affirming.

BEING A GRACE-GIVER

Dr. Catherine Hart Weber, therapist and author of *Is Your Teen Stressed or Depressed?* told me, "My daughter has been through major hair traumas." Although Catherine suggested it wasn't the best idea, Nicole took her naturally blond hair to a cosmetology school stylist and asked for one of the two-toned colors she'd seen in a magazine. The young woman bleached the top and dyed the bottom part of her hair jet black, leaving her with a distinct skunk look. Nicole came home, cried her eyes out, and couldn't go anywhere for fear of ridicule.

Catherine could have overreacted with, "I told you so! Why did you do this?" Instead, she gave her daughter grace by responding, "It's fixable; it's not the end of the world! I know you're upset, but it's just *hair.* Let's see what we can do."

"As moms, we've got to give grace and practice the art of detachment," Catherine says. "Be connected in love and caring, but realize that if they choose in their journey to have purple hair, it's no reflection on us." Many women continue to experiment with their style into adulthood as their identity develops, their careers change. Accept those changes. And if the appearance your daughter chooses isn't your preference, hold it lightly and detach with love.

FOCUS ON WHAT MATTERS

Maggie got a tattoo in her freshman year at the University of Colorado in Boulder. When her mom, Mary Ann, came to visit, she saw her friend Libby's tattoo first.

"*You* don't have one, *do you*?" Mary Ann inquired.

Then her daughter showed her the little rose tattoo on the inside of her ankle. Mary Ann wasn't crazy about it but stayed calm and didn't say much. To her generation, tattoos were associated with a certain class of people, and she doesn't like the idea of defacing the body God gave you. "Graffiti on a building you can paint over, but tattoos are permanent," she told me. Though she was disappointed about the decision (and that she wasn't consulted), she thanked God it was small, especially when Maggie's cousin got a big frog tattoo on her back a few months later.

Mary Ann's attitude of accepting and loving her daughter unconditionally helped immensely when the next year her daughter decided to get a nose ring. Maggie had come back from Colorado to attend the University of Oklahoma and didn't want to conform to the preppy OU look. She wanted to express her individuality. After seeing her daughter struggle with depression the summer before, Mary Ann was just glad to see her happy and doing well in her studies. So she was quite willing to let the other things, the "externals" slide. Mom didn't overreact, and the nose ring was short-lived.

Tattoos aren't our generation's favorite accessory. "How do you think that butterfly tattoo is going to look as it moves down your waist when you get older?" one mom asked her daughter. Another said, "Tattooing your whole arm is fine if you're a Maori warrior."

I too have struggled with the idea of body art because it was foreign to Baby Boomers like me. From talking with twenty- and thirty-something women, I've come to realize they often have a very symbolic, personal meaning. Amanda, twenty-six, showed me her tattoos and explained: "This one is in memory of a close friend who passed away, and the other two (a cat and a swirling artistic design) are just my own creative self-expression."

Ashley, her friend said, "The cross is for my dad. Here's my mom's handwriting that says, 'Reach for the stars and never settle for less.' And the angel wings are for my grandma who had a heart attack and almost died."

What could I say? Though it wasn't my style of commemorating someone I loved, these expressions were heartfelt and meant a great deal to these women. I don't know how their moms felt about their daughters' body art, but as for me, I want to choose relationship over appearances—don't you?

A Daughter's Perspective

My mom and I have varying ideas regarding style. I am not my mom! I am my own person, with my own style, my own tastes, my own opinions and thoughts. Not only of my hair, but my look, my clothes, my emerging identity. When I was sixteen, mom "released my hair" and let me do whatever I wanted with it. Before then it was a power struggle. I wanted to do something different to it, and she wanted it to stay the same. It was a big step for her to give up control and let me dye it burgundy or cut it short. But it helped me find out who I was apart from her. We started being able to agree to disagree on our different opinions regarding style and expression. And I appreciated her realization that there were a lot of more important issues in our relationship.

Flash forward to my twenties and beyond. I love change. My mom balks at it. My belief is that every woman should shake her look up every once in a while. I think change invigorates the soul and can even spice up a mood or relationship. I don't know if this personal opinion has more to do with being a daughter or having been a hairstylist, but I've seen change work in these ways time after time, both personally and for others. Different looks express different feelings, moods, career paths, and personal viewpoints. I think this describes how my generation views beauty: Change is good; expression through fashion, tattooing, and hairstyles is healthy and beautiful. We see fashion and body art as a creative outlet. We even want our moms to invest in their own changing look to find their beauty and bliss.

Take jeans for example. To me, jeans are an expression of what I'm feeling that day, whereas my mother usually wears the same type of "mom jeans." I have low-rise and skinny jeans for those days when I feel a little edgy, and I don my environmentally friendly TOMS shoes and long tunic T-shirt. I wear the jeans, I feel the mood, and creatively I feel alive. Another day I might feel a bit "granola girl" and wear bell-bottoms that are a little loose and hippy. Add a worn peasant shirt and my mood feels comfy and natural. Perhaps this sounds a little melodramatic, but it can give you some insight into what might seem insignificant to you— like a pair of jeans—but is significant to your daughter.

Daughters want to hear that we are accepted as we are, not if we change into what you think is more feminine or professional or suitable for whatever phase we might be in. We want to know your love and opinion of us isn't based on whether we got a tattoo or never wear dresses to church. We want to feel comfortable in our own skin just as you do in yours, and we sometimes get tired of the focus being so external.

I know my mom probably thought, *What the heck is she thinking?* during my many style changes and phases of looks. But she did a great job of not saying so out loud. After my rocky teens, I felt like she was my biggest fan of changing looks, almost as if she was entertained by what color and style was going to come next. She complimented me and embraced me for who I was. So I felt free to be who I was, and that still holds true today.

Her openness toward my self-expression through style and change helps me feel closer to her. With all the issues we had through the years, this was one area in which she "got" me, even as intrinsically different as we are. I have a need to creatively evolve; it's a value to me in life. Even if she doesn't have the same need, Mom has embraced this facet of me, and in that I feel accepted.

Now, the highest compliment she can give me is asking for my input when she's trying to pick out a new pair of jeans or lets me do her hair and makeup. I realize I'm not the fashionista of the world, and I don't pretend to have some superior style to my mom. I appreciate our differences. But it feels incredible when my mom affirms my skills or strengths as a stylist or student of fashion by asking for my input and letting me bring those skills to the table.

Mom and I aren't the only ones who struggle with comparison. As women we innately, biologically struggle with self-image issues through much of our life. As daughters we grow up comparing ourselves to our mothers but also to our siblings—especially if those siblings are sisters. When we feel that we are being compared as sisters one to another, it can be tremendously hurtful throughout our adult lives.

I didn't grow up with sisters, but as Mom shared, I learned how to compare myself to friends and cousins that fit more into my definition of beautiful. I used to think how wrong Mom was in her assessment of herself. In my eyes, she was beautiful, strong, active, and smart. She had no idea at the time that I defined myself by the measuring stick of "plain" that was used in her family when it came to physical acceptance.

Though my parents were both quite affirming of me at every stage, I still felt my dishwater-blond hair wasn't pretty. Our experience of talking about this was one of the most enlightening, bonding conversations we've had. Now in my thirties, we were finally able to talk openly and honestly about our combined lack of self-esteem based on faulty perception. All family systems have quirks and brokenness galore, ours included, but the issue, once faced, was what drew my mom and me closer together.

We've learned how to laugh about our similar negative talk about things like hair color and texture. Now we purposefully try to encourage each other to accept our own "inner diva" and revel in our beauty because we are finally attempting to conquer that monster called comparison—together. Nothing is more bonding than being able to laugh off some of our biggest hang-ups—especially when it comes to our appearance.

Two-Part Harmony

As Ali and I talked together about how mothers could let go of their expectations and embrace their daughters' unique looks, one thing that seemed clear was this: focus on some specific, positive aspects of your daughter's appearance—because the truth is, "She doesn't want your advice. She wants your blessing."[5]

Ask yourself: What can I admire about my daughter's unique appearance and beauty or her style preferences? As you think about what you appreciate, make a point to affirm her in that quality, perhaps write her a note about it. Are there other ways you could make her feel celebrated, validated?

It's also helpful to think back on your own life and remember your attempt to break out of the mold, to do something different than your mom, sister, or peers. Perhaps take a friend out and try to get some conversation going about your experiences—like whether you changed clothes and hairstyles often or found a comfortable rut and stayed there. Discuss whether you were affirmed or criticized by your own mother. Pondering this can help you get into your daughter's shoes and better understand where she's coming from on appearance issues. It can possibly even transform your relationship.

However you've related to your daughter and appearance issues, you can form new patterns by becoming a woman who is at peace with yourself both inside and out. Rather than nagging or criticizing about what your daughter eats or whether she exercises, you can be a positive example.

As mothers, we can look at what might be perceived by our society or by us as "defects" or imperfections, and realize those very qualities are evidence of a person's individuality. And most of all, we can remember that our daughters are not a reflection of ourselves and that when we let our daughters be themselves, we gain more harmony in the relationship.

TOO CLOSE FOR COMFORT

• • • • •

If you recognize that you are overly dependent upon
people, or if you find yourself regularly inviting or
attracting people to depend on you, understand that
God did not intend for people to continuously
depend on other people for their well-being. As we
mature, he wants us to depend upon him.
—LESLIE VERNICK, *THE EMOTIONALLY DESTRUCTIVE RELATIONSHIP*

• • • • •

There are lots of positive things about being good friends with
your daughter. I've talked to moms who say their adult daughter is their very closest, best friend. They shop together and tell each other
everything. We all want connection with our daughters. But when Mom
sees her daughter as her main confidante or they become overly close, it
can hinder a healthy transition to adulthood. That was the case for Julie.

Julie and her mother had always been close. Yet from high school on,
her biggest struggle was that her mom was so involved in her life it was
suffocating. She appreciated and loved her mom, but during the college
years she wanted a little distance to grow. But her mom kept needing to be
needed. She was dependent on her daughter's dependency, which fostered
insecurity in Julie. This sweet, caring mother had done *everything* for her
daughter when she lived at home and then kept doing *everything* even

through her twenties (her taxes, reconciling her checkbook, and doing her laundry, all of which Julie was capable of doing herself). "You're so busy; come home this weekend and I'll get it all done." Her mom did all this with the best of intentions, and she expected *a lot* from her daughter in return.

Julie's dad had been emotionally absent early on, so as a child Julie was expected to be her mom's listener. Hers was the shoulder her mother cried on when she was upset. Being mom's main emotional support felt spiritual and noble, especially when she had to sacrifice some of her own fun times with friends, but it was actually detrimental to the process of Julie's learning to grow up and live her own life. Their too-close relationship sabotaged Julie's individuation, the primary developmental task of young adulthood.

When she started pulling away in small steps during college, like spending the weekend on campus for an activity with friends, her mom asked guilt-producing questions like, "Why aren't you coming home more?" or "Are your friends more fun than I am?"

Being a compliant people pleaser, Julie got sucked into an enmeshed relationship with her mother. She gave up a lot of her own perfectly normal desires and interests in order to go home when her mom needed companionship or to call her more often than she had time for.

Julie's mom didn't realize she was manipulating situations and thereby preventing her daughter from being a stable, healthy adult. Mom's hyperinvolvement eventually not only hurt Julie's ability to feel good about herself and live her own life, it also hurt their relationship.

Consequently, while her greatest wish was for her daughter to get married, Julie's mother didn't realize her overinvolvement was a big part of the reason her daughter wasn't developing a relationship with a guy. When Julie didn't marry through her twenties and early thirties, her mom asked from time to time, out of real concern, "Don't you want to get married?" This is never a good question for us to ask.

Mom and daughter operated in this kind of dysfunctional connection for a decade before Julie realized the growing venom and resentment she felt toward her mom. She'd started avoiding her, and when they were together, Julie was either curt or silent. Then Julie sought counseling to find a way to detach with love, forgive, and live her own life while still honoring her mother.

At first her mother resisted the change in their relationship. She cried, balked, and felt sorry for herself. But as Julie stood her ground and learned how to separate and draw some healthy boundaries, her mother finally got the message: She needed to have her own life, not try to live through her daughter. She got involved in a Bible study and community projects, participating in life on her own for a change. Through those groups, she made some new friends.

As Julie and her mom created some space from each other, their mother-daughter relationship became more open, and what her mother had longed for happened: Julie drew close and began to enjoy her mom more than ever—quite a contrast to spending time with her because she felt obligated to. That's what happens when we allow our daughters to grow into the adults they're supposed to be. Then they are free to return on their own timetable.

Just as Julie and her mom experienced from establishing boundaries, our relationships with our own daughters will actually be much healthier and the time we do spend together more enjoyable if we do the same.

BREAKING UNHEALTHY TIES

In her book *The Emotionally Destructive Relationship,* Leslie Vernick points out the following signs of a too close, emotionally destructive relationship: one person is regularly overprotective, overbearing—or both—toward the other; one person is overdependent upon the other to affirm her personal value and worth and meet all her needs; one person exhibits chronic indifference, neglect, or both toward the thoughts, feelings, or well-being of the other.[1]

When Ali and I interviewed daughters, we heard this "too-close" scenario often and discovered that Julie's story was not an isolated one. When moms use their daughters as soul mates/sole confidantes or are overly dependent, it creates an unhealthy tie that is very hard for the daughters to break. These ties don't build an enjoyable relationship between mother and daughter but instead cause the daughter to pull away or seethe quietly with resentment. When she does draw the line, it tends to come with guilt, worry, and anger toward her mom.

If you sense your daughter and you have been a bit too close for comfort or you're dissatisfied with her distance, maybe it's time to reconnect with yourself. Take some time to get to know yourself better and identify your hopes and dreams, your "bucket list" of things you want to do while you're still on this side of the grass. Get comfortable with just being with *yourself*, journaling your thoughts and feelings, and being fine with solitude.

And make time to cultivate your own friendships. That's one of the best things we moms can do for our daughters, especially during the college and twenty-something years when our daughter's developmental task is to separate from us. We can share thoughts and appropriate feelings, of course, but it's not a daughter's job to be the repository of intimate details of your life. It's vital to avoid confiding to her toxic feelings about her father (or another family member) that will negatively affect her relationship with the person. It's not her job to be your therapist. That's too heavy a burden to bear, and she's not trained for counseling yet anyway.

When you shape her into that role, it brings turmoil during a formative stage of her life and can mess up her own sense of identity and sexuality—both of which can take years in therapy to resolve. She's still your daughter, and you are *not* her little girl. If you don't switch the roles, the relationship will be healthier—and isn't that what you want? Your daughter will be freer to live her life and develop her own identity, friendships, and interests. And as you are available without hovering and detached without cutting her off, she'll have the emotional energy she needs for learning and tackling the normal challenges of her adult years.

HEALTHY ADULT FRIENDSHIPS

- Instead of making your daughter the center of your life or only confidante—think of her as an adult friend among your other friends.

- Steer away from micromanaging her appearance, eating, or social life. You wouldn't do that to a friend.

- When she indicates a need for space, respect it and know you'll come together at a different time.

- Instead of looking at your daughter's independence as rejection, see it as a feather in your cap.

- Be direct and honest about how you feel about your relationship, but be ready and willing to hear direct and honest perspective. Remember, *it's a duet—not a solo.*

As mothers, when we find our own best friends (in addition to close communication with our husbands, if they are in the picture), it doesn't diminish our relationship with our daughter. It enhances our bond with her. We need women we can confide in and trust because developing connections with other women is part of taking care of ourselves. In the process, we not only have an opportunity to be deeply honest with someone who is better equipped to support us, but we get to have fun too. In chapter 12, "Taking Care of Yourself," we discuss this in greater detail.

ALLEVIATING HER CONCERNS

Many daughters are burdened about their parents. Georgia Shaffer, a Pennsylvania-licensed psychologist and author of *How Not to Date a Loser: A Guide to Making Smart Choices,* told me recently that one of the main reasons young women come to campus counseling centers is that they are worried about problems their moms and dads are having back at home.

As I wrote earlier, Ali and I had an unhealthy pattern of excessive concern for each other—me for her depression and she for almost everything going on with her dad and me. I had some friends when she left home, so I didn't depend on her for that, even though I wanted to be closer to her. But I didn't spend enough time with my friends. Like many of you, I worked too much and played too little. With the demands I faced, I didn't feel I could set aside a lot of time to socialize with them. Besides, the disease of alcoholism that intruded on our family carries with it the element of isolation, and I was often caught in that.

Since Ali wasn't being chummy with me, I knew I couldn't count on her for my social needs (nor on my quiet, loving husband or on our sons, who were also growing up). So I started a writing critique group with others in the publishing industry. I took a weekend trip with two girlfriends. I began to make time to meet my friend Marcy at Starbucks. Those were good steps that made Ali feel she was off the hook, so to speak.

I know now that Ali was anxious about her father and me far too much—that was part of our enmeshed "too closeness." She's always been empathetic and sensitive to the emotions of those around her, and worrying about us drained energy she needed for her own life. While it is unhealthy to dump our negative emotions on our kids, it is healthy to let them know the truth, especially if it affects them. I regret that in spite of our best efforts and my attempts at keeping a positive attitude, we gave Ali cause for concern by not talking with her about what was happening. The anxiety she felt drained the spirit she needed for the big challenges she was facing as a young woman.

The good news is that whether we are forty-five or sixty-something, it's not too late to face our own issues, find healing for our inner pain, cultivate new friends and, as my daughter says, "Get a life," so our daughters can go on with theirs.

A Daughter's Perspective

I see the way I pushed and tugged away from mom all those years, how much tension my silence and sometimes disdain felt to her, hurt her. I get a pang in my thirty-three-year-old heart just thinking about it—a heart that used to beat so shallowly about her. That said, I get it now. We still have our irksome moments with each other, but understanding, empathy, and newfound gratitude for all she was and did and is supersedes the negative things I used to hyperfocus on.

I understand now the constant challenge of having to reassess your involvement and closeness to your child. I have begun to experience that tightrope of control and letting go with my two sons, though they are in their early elementary years. It's painful beyond words at times. I get that now.

Then, I didn't get it. Most of us daughters don't get it when we've not had the "coming back" to you yet. All I knew then was that I wanted not just my freedom to find my identity, but I wanted to know my mom wanted me to find it too. I wanted desperately to hear her say, "I believe you can do this adult thing, Ali; I believe you are the author of your destiny now, not me… So go for it! Experience life; really live; don't be afraid to make mistakes. I did; we all did. Just go be you, unapologetically! I believe in you, and I'm not going to worry about you."

So when I say I longed to hear those words from my mom, I mean I *needed* to hear them. I needed to know that it was good and normal to separate myself from her and not have to follow her path and be able to own my life and essentially become a healthy, responsible adult. I also needed to know that she was okay and that Dad was okay. I knew he drank too much, and I could see the strain it caused on my mom. I was worried about her health and just wanted to talk about the stresses openly and honestly.

When moms try to be too close, daughters try that much harder to separate from them (and possibly resent them that much more). The individuating process is the most normal, needed process of our lives, so we hope you'll support it. It sets the course for our adulthood and all that comes with that. A strong sense of self and confidence in who God has made us to be (not who Mom or Dad has made us to be) is the goal of our lives as we venture into independence and adulthood. We daughters need desperately to know you aren't dying to keep us young and close but that you *want us* to develop emotionally into adulthood and become healthy, responsible adults—not fearful, reticent women who need, need, need.

It's so good for us daughters when our moms take care of themselves—especially in their marriage. Because then we see you as a better role model and want to be more like you, or want to be closer at some point.

Two-Part Harmony

Take heart, Mom. One day your daughter will have a life of her own, managing her own children or an office full of people, or maybe she'll even be president of the United States. She will learn to give grace and forgiveness—and maybe ask for it too. And as she does, she will come to appreciate you and all the complexities that surrounded your mothering her.

Here's what we're learning as we've talked to many mothers: It comes down to a balance—not a disconnected, I'm-too-busy-for-you stance or a too-close-for-comfort, enmeshed relationship with our daughter. Let her know you're there for her when she needs someone to talk to, and then listen well when she takes you up on the offer. Invite her to meet you at a coffee shop, and don't take it personally if she's not able to fit that into her schedule. Be her greatest encourager in all the steps along the way as she becomes a full-fledged adult. And while you're at it, enjoy the freedom to have a life of your own.

RESPECT AND BELIEF

• • • • •

Is any other relationship as complex, unbreakable,
loving, disappointing, temper-tossed, life-shaping,
and downright in-each-other's hair as the one
between the two of you?

—OPRAH WINFREY

• • • • •

Jane's mom still tries to keep a tight grip on control even though her daughter has a full-time job and is responsible. The twenty-five-year-old is temporarily living at home while saving money for a deposit on her own house and paying off student loans. One day Jane stopped by for a short lunch break before returning to the bank where she works in the investments department.

Just minutes after Jane sat down to eat her turkey sandwich, her mom asked, "Don't you need to get back to work? You had a doctor's appointment yesterday. You don't want to make your boss think you're not giving it your all or putting in enough hours."

Jane fumed. "You don't have to tell me what to do, Mom. I have my schedule right here in my BlackBerry, and I'm always at work on time. You don't need to tell me things I already know." Every time her mom questions her judgment or behavior, Jane feels disrespected and reacts in anger. "Why can't you believe I can handle things and know what to do? I'm an adult."

Natalie feels she's never been able to mesh well with her mom like her sister has. "I want to be closer to my mom, but she's distant and so am I," she said. "The one thing I wish is that she would respect me. She loves me; don't get me wrong. But she rarely listens to me or gives me her attention when I try to talk to her. Mostly I got lectures when I was a teenager, and I still do even though I'm a mom myself now."

Natalie and her four-year-old moved back in with her parents temporarily while her husband was deployed. Whenever she tried to have a conversation with her mother, her sister or dad would interrupt, and that was the end of it. Mom questioned why she didn't choose to baptize her son in their denominational tradition and why she wasn't taking him to Sunday school. And she wouldn't listen when Natalie tried to explain her reasons.

After two months and two big fights with her mom, Natalie moved out. "If I ever have an adult daughter, one thing I'm going to be sure to do is listen to her and respect her even if she thinks differently about things than me," she told me. "It's hard for me to respect her because *I* don't feel respected."

What is this "respect" these daughters are longing for? Why did it make them so mad that their moms weren't giving it? According to Webster's, *respect* means the act of giving someone particular attention and consideration. It means esteeming our daughter to show with our words and actions that she has value.

As these illustrations show, when adult daughters don't feel respected by their mothers, they get angry—deeply angry. Though they may express their anger in different ways, the lack of respect usually leads to tension and conflict in the relationship.

Women seek respect because it's wrapped up with their self-esteem and feeling of worth and value. As one daughter said, "We talk about it a lot, we yearn for it, we expect it, and we notice when we haven't been given it by others." In relationships, respect goes right along with love and commitment.

Practically speaking, to respect your adult daughter means to:

Acknowledge that her opinions have value, even if you don't agree with them. That way, you can disagree about an issue and still have harmony in your relationship. The opposite, disrespecting response when your daughter shares an opinion is to say, "You're wrong," and then expound on your opinion. Just as you wouldn't discount or devalue a good friend's thoughts and ideas, your daughter deserves the same kindness. Maybe even tell her you appreciate her courage in taking a stand on an issue. If you're going to share your thoughts, attempt to understand where she's coming from first by asking, "Could you tell me more about that?" or "How'd you arrive at that conclusion?"

Show your daughter common courtesy, just as you would want to be treated or as you'd treat any other adult. When we're upset or feel hurt, we can handle it in a calm, private manner instead of loudly upbraiding our daughters or making them the target of jokes in front of friends or family members.

Listen to her. Although we're going into more detail about communication in the next chapter, part of showing respect is listening to someone. Whether an adult or child, when a person is listened to, she feels valued and respected.

Be sensitive to your daughter's feelings and thoughts, and don't minimize or ignore them. Here's where I fell down on the job! I thought I was respecting my daughter because we showed her and her brothers a lot of courtesy growing up. We purposed to respect their opinions and listen to their different perspectives. However, I didn't value Ali's negative feelings and negative thoughts as much as her positive ones. I'd say things like,

"Oh honey, let's look on the bright side…," and that hurt her feelings. It also made her angry and resentful.

The more I didn't accept or tried to change my daughter's feelings, the more she hid them and sunk deeper into unhealthy coping skills. I didn't know that letting her emote either positive or negative was showing respect. Or that ignoring or trying to change someone's emotional state—*especially* if it's depression—is invalidating and leads to the person feeling unaccepted.

Ali and I were sometimes doing a dance to two totally different songs at the same time and would collide in our ability to show respect and feel respected by the other. Maybe I didn't accept the full spectrum of my daughter with all her dark and light moods because I was afraid of what I didn't understand. This created palpable tension at times, and I didn't know what to do with her strong emotions or choices.

RESPECTING OUR DAUGHTERS BEFORE THEY GET IT TOGETHER

All daughters—whether they're succeeding or struggling, whether they've chosen a career path or are avoiding commitment to any stable job, whether they're regrouping after a divorce or have been through a string of broken relationships, whether they share our religious beliefs or don't—need their moms' respect and belief. Not after they have everything figured out, are out of their crisis, or are achieving something noteworthy. But right where they are. Even if they need help but aren't seeking it yet.

That's what one mom I know is learning to do with Deborah, her twenty-something daughter who moved back home because her finances had fallen apart. Concerned with Deborah's self-destructive tendencies, which included smoking, drinking, and getting involved in toxic relationships, Mom welcomed her in but shared her concerns saying, "I think this is an opportunity for you to get your life in order—to begin making healthier choices." Although that comment didn't bring about overnight change, Mom has set a few boundaries: no smoking or drinking at home, and Deborah had to get a job, help out around the house, and contribute to the grocery fund.

At the same time, Mom continues to express belief in her daughter by saying things like:

- "I love you, and I believe there's a healthier you in there, the real you."
- "I believe you're going to figure your way out."
- "You're worthy of love." (Particularly important affirmation because her heart has been broken several times.)
- "You're capable of great things."

This mother is not waiting until Deborah is doing those great things; she's treating her with grace right where she is. She's not withholding belief in God's love and good plan for her daughter until she's got it together spiritually. Even as she keeps handing Deborah over to God and holding her accountable to the boundaries she set, this mom's words and behavior project positive expectations for her daughter. Instead of, "You're not going to amount to anything if you keep doing what you're doing," Deborah hears, "I believe in you."

SEEKING MOM'S APPROVAL

Remember how you longed for your mother's approval when you were young? For her to say, "Good job!" when you brought home your report card, or for her to compliment the zany outfit you had put together in the fifth grade? For her to affirm you, when as a teenager you were in school and working a part-time job, or you wanted to hear something positive from her about the guy you were dating (thus approving of your choice)?

Whether an adult daughter admits it or not, a mom's approval and affirmation is vital at various stages along the journey.

So what happens and how do they feel if they'd don't get it? "Approval-seeking leads to constant struggle," said Rosalind C. Barnett in her research study, "Adult Daughters and Their Mothers: Harmony or Hostility?" "Trying to please one's mother and being angry for not pleasing go hand-in-hand."[1] That's why your daughter needs your respect and validation, *especially* if she's making different choices than you would have her make.

Not that it's always easy. When a daughter pursues a different lifestyle or religious or political path and you don't agree with her, it can be a struggle to accept her, much less affirm her. Yet that's the most relationship building thing you can do. That's what Jan discovered when her oldest daughter married and moved to California. Her younger daughter chose a traditional route, got married in her twenties, stayed near the family, and was a stay-at-home mom of two children, which pleased Jan to no end.

But Amy's choices did not. Jan's older, independent daughter had an advanced degree, and both she and her husband had fabulous, high-pressure careers and a life they loved. She and her husband decided they didn't want to have any children; they just didn't fit in with their goals.

Jan struggled with the reality that Amy wouldn't have any kids. She worried that Amy would be alone if her husband died before she did since he was older and pointed that out to her. But after a few conversations, Jan realized it wouldn't do any good to try to pressure her daughter to have kids anyway. Knowing her nature, Jan figured she'd think, "Now I definitely *won't* do it." And then Amy would alienate her.

"I think you'd be great parents," Jan told Amy one day when she was visiting, "but it's your decision. It's your life and we respect your decision."

That was a turning point. Even though they live more than a thousand miles from each other and couldn't be more different, because of the acceptance and respect of her daughter's choice, Jan's respect tore down some of the walls Amy had built up between them. Now Amy calls and talks to her mom about anything. When Jan and her husband visit twice a year, Amy and her husband are wonderful hosts and the door's always open. Jan knows she'd much rather have the relationship than try to be "right" or convince Amy that her sister's and mom's way of doing life—with children—is somehow better than what her daughter has chosen.

While a mom can advise (with caution and sensitivity), it's the adult daughter's part to make her own decisions and know that we won't come back and say, "I told you so," if she makes a mistake or things go awry. And when

- your daughter comes home with a potential mate you doubt would be an ideal life partner...
- her career track isn't the same as yours...
- your value systems collide...

Instead of throwing up your hands and completely detaching, you can speak the truth without judgment, drop your own agenda, and open yourself to your daughter's heart.

Maybe your daughter's personality drives you crazy. Maybe she's always pushing your buttons or she exhausts you. If your daughter seems perpetually angry, it's helpful to consider what's underneath the anger. Ask, "Is there something you'd like to talk about?" If she jabs at you or is disrespectful to you, call her on it and set a boundary: "You're speaking disrespectfully to me, and I'm not going to tolerate it. When you're ready to speak civilly to me, I'll be open to listen... I don't want to give you practice being disrespectful. It's not a skill you need for life, and I'd be doing you a disservice to allow you to continue."

• A Daughter's Perspective •

As I've talked to many other daughters, I hear over and over how, like me, they just want to know that their moms like them. We daughters hope you'll validate and affirm us simply because of who we are, not because we have our life together, but because we're on the journey and doing the best we can, whether it looks like it or not. We feel respected and believed in when you still want to get to know us, not when you draw assumptions of us.

Daughters seem to be saying, "Come meet us where we are, ask us questions, let us see your human side and let us show you ours. Consider respecting us even if you don't see the whole picture and don't understand us yet. Embrace that we are human and make mistakes, just as you do." Closeness can emerge when we least expect it, particularly as mothers and daughters find their way to acceptance of each other. And through acceptance we can find mutual respect.

The need for respect is as universal as the need for love. When you accept us, we daughters feel respected. Acceptance feels like love and care and freedom to be who we are. When you listen to our opinion, we feel respected by you—even more so when you are curious enough to ask us if you don't understand. We feel respected when you treat us as your equal, not your subordinate. When you don't make assumptions about the phase we are in or our social group or who we date or marry, we feel respected. We feel respected when you legitimately enjoy our presence and just want to be in the moment with us. (We don't feel respected when you have an agenda and list of things you want to tell us or convince us about when we hang out together.) We feel respected when you say you're sorry when you're wrong instead of thinking an apology is a sign of weakness for a parent. We think it's a strength. How do you think we learn how to respect others and apologize when we are wrong? You're our best role model.

Someone asked me once, "Do you want to be right, or do you want to be happy?" Until I heard that wise phrase, I never realized that sometimes I've insisted on my rightness to the point of utter unhappiness in relationships. I've done it with my mom, and she with me. And two unhappy people attached to their "rightness" make little room for mutual respect.

We feel respect when you don't push a subject if we've communicated we don't want to go there. We feel respect when you give us the freedom to choose to share or not share with you. And when we do share something personal with you, don't tell any other members of the family or your friends, so we can trust that what's shared with you stays with you. When we feel you respect us, we will trust you, and we'll probably open up more when we feel safe and accepted.

We want mutual respect as much as you do. Respect boosts our self-worth. The opposite—disrespect—breaks us down and makes us doubt ourselves. Will you listen without reacting? When you do, it feels to us like comfort and acceptance. When you listen respectfully, we're not afraid of being judged or discounted. We aren't afraid of you and what you might say or do when we open up our lives to you. We don't want you to give up all your beliefs, thoughts, opinions; we respect those as yours. We celebrate them. Just don't project them onto us! Please respect our need to establish our own beliefs, thoughts, and opinions.

Let's talk instead of disconnecting when we don't understand each other. Please don't assume anything; just ask. Dialogue helps us feel respected. We can't make each other change, so doesn't that put us in a good place to try to get to know each other and keep getting to know each other throughout our lives?

There's nothing like feeling your mom believes in you and is proud of you, no matter how different you may be from her or how far you've moved, what job you've taken or who you've ended up with (or not ended up with). One of the most significant things my mom has done for years has been writing notes and poems to me. She started long ago and filled her messages with encouragement, hope, and dreams for me, even when I didn't have any hope or dreams for myself. She wrote to me and translated her heart through the words. Amazingly, she passed a tradition on to me without my even knowing it.

It's a battle for us daughters to act civil, sweet, and overtly grateful when we feel we're not living up to our mom's expectations. We get frustrated with feeling that we're letting down the one person we want to get oodles of affirmation from. We revert to a kind of adolescent response to our moms, which makes it difficult to communicate anything positive. It's just a season or stage most often, but respect along with gratitude, I've discovered, can help bridge the gap.

Two-Part Harmony

What if, instead of focusing on what you don't like in your daughter or what's lacking in the relationship, you chose to focus on your daughter's good qualities, the unique things you love about her, and the strengths in your mother-daughter connection?

"When we focus on the negative, it only provokes more negative emotions in the emotional brain," psychologist and mother Catherine Hart Weber told me one day as we talked. "But when we express appreciation to someone, the chemical in the brain associated with happiness is released," she added. Those positive emotions motivate the person and even enhance her relationships.

"Focus on what God can do, what he *is doing* and what you're thankful for," Catherine suggested. "Your daughter doesn't need to keep hearing 'here's what's wrong with you'; she wants to hear 'this is what is right with you and what I love and appreciate.' We do that best when our minds are already focused in that direction."

Her advice reminded me of how The Message paraphrases Philippians 4:8–9, which I would call *very good words for mothers of adult daughters:* "Summing it all up, friends, I'd say you'll do best by filling your minds and meditating on things true, noble, reputable, authentic, compelling, gracious—the best, not the worst; the beautiful, not the ugly; things to praise, not things to curse.... Do that, and God, who makes everything work together, will work you into his most excellent harmonies."

You may only see small glimpses of these true, gracious qualities. Other times you may be thinking, *Who is this person? Who's taken over my daughter's body? She's changed so much and I don't know if I like the changes.* That's the time to start a gratitude list specifically about your daughter.

There are no rules, just a bulleted list will do. You can be at home or at a coffee shop, and get out a little spiral notebook when you're spiraling into disappointment about what your daughter's not doing or how she's just said something that ruined your day. Just write down the first grateful thoughts that come to mind, and those thoughts will exponentially increase. As they do, you may find the negative ones will dissipate.

This is an active way to open your heart to the good in your daughter or to any other part of your life you've been unhappy with. Remember that she's a *gift*, no matter how she's acting right now. And what's the best response to a gift? *Gratitude.* By seeing her as the gift she is now and not as someone who needs to be changed, then you can release and enjoy your daughter in deeper ways. Gratitude will soften your heart toward her, and your words and actions will follow, ultimately leading to a stronger connection between you and your daughter.

COMMUNICATION

* * * * *

Women are healed by, or ache for, satisfying conversations with their mothers and grown daughters, in
some cases to build on already excellent relationships, in others to break out of cycles of misunderstanding that can turn amiable conversations into
painful or angry ones in the blink of an eye.

—DEBORAH TANNEN, *YOU'RE WEARING THAT?*

* * * * *

One evening a few months ago, Ali was studying at Barnes &
Noble. I was surprised when she called and said she wanted a
study break. Would I go to the movie with her? I drove the fifteen minutes to meet her at the bookstore. I expected we'd chat before heading
over to the theater; I do enjoy connecting with her and catching up on
each other's lives.

But she had different ideas. After a few attempts to stir up conversations to which she responded a bit huffy, I realized she was just in a melan-
choly mood and wanted to read magazines. She thought I could read her
mind about this. Our wires were crossed, and we had different expectations but didn't express them. We ended up with hurt feelings that
evening and a while later sat silently through the movie. Afterward, we
went our separate ways.

Just as I did, mothers and daughters of all ages reach for connection. Yet even with sincere intentions, some of our attempts to converse with them end in a misunderstanding or conflict—which was not at all what we had in mind.

That wasn't the only day communication got frustrating for Ali and me. Other times I gave unwanted snippets of advice. Or at times she sensed my anxiety and stress about a minicrisis she had just shared, putting the focus on my feelings and need to "fix" the situation rather than trusting that she would figure it out on her own. Some days she was sleep deprived or hormonal, so it was more about *how she felt* than what I said or did. Sometimes I was grumpy or we were both under pressure from other directions, other times I finished her sentence—which daughters find irritating—or didn't pay attention to what she was saying because I was cooking a meal.

Can you relate? Ever try to give a gentle suggestion or bring up a subject and your daughter replied curtly, "Mom, we've already talked about this. *So don't go there.*" Perhaps this was right after she told you, "Mom, yellow is not a good color on you" or "your skirt is too long."

"A mother said of her grown daughter, 'Our conversations are the best and the worst of all possible conversations,'"[1] observed Deborah Tannen. Maybe that's because though we long to have a good conversation, sometimes without realizing it we say the very things that derail communication. That's why in this chapter we're going to look at some of the ways to foster and improve our communication, such as letting go of expectations, leaving the past behind, sharing our flaws, and listening actively. Take heart, if your conversations have been strained in the past, know that it's not too late to turn things around.

Sometimes it's not just the words we say but our underlying expectations that are a barrier to good communication.

WHAT DAUGHTERS ARE SAYING

It is possible that our daughters may be misinterpreting or overreacting to what we say, but it's helpful to look at their point of view. Here are some things daughters say about conversation with their moms:

- "When my mom and I talk on the phone, she starts in on her litany of things to be afraid of— the *E. coli* in my spinach, the danger of going to the mall by myself, taking birth control pills that cause cancer. It's just draining to listen to her."

- "My parents live in Seattle, but I chose to live in Portland because they get on my nerves, especially my mom who *always* finds something to criticize or complain about."

- "When I tell Mom I found another job possibility on Monster.com, she says, 'Why do you keep looking for a job in Chicago? Des Moines is such a great place to live. Look how nice it was for you to grow up here.'"

- "When I visited recently, Mom said, 'You've lost weight.' I was so pleased, but before I could say thanks, she said with a coy smile, 'But I'm still the smallest.' She was being sarcastic, and it stung."

- "My mom calls me almost every day and gives me advice I haven't asked for. If I don't do things her way she gets angry. She treats me like I'm sixteen—and I'm thirty-five."

Changing Our Expectations

During a daughter's adult years, moms often expect the relationship to be a two-way street and want regular chats to continue as they did when she lived at home. However, most out-of-the-nest girls are *not thinking about their moms* nearly as much as their mothers are thinking about them. They have a lot on their minds: a new campus or city, or the business world to navigate, roommates to adjust to, new friends and relationships with guys—or the longing for one.

You may want to touch base by phone daily or talk more often than your daughter does. Perhaps when you call, she's busy cramming for finals or racing off to work. Or she's changing a messy diaper or in the middle of making dinner and the kids are screaming—not the best time for a talk. First communication tip: don't take it personally; it doesn't help your connection.

As I've talked to women, I've found it's not unusual for expectations to fuel a misunderstanding when our daughters' expectations and ours don't match up. Here's one of those situations a daughter told me about:

> When my little brother flew into town, he wanted me to pick him up at the airport. When Mom heard about it, she asked me, "Why doesn't he want me to pick him up? Let's all go down, your sisters and kids, and then we can all go eat and to a movie."
>
> I didn't want to be squished in the backseat with the kids' car seats so I said, "You can go get him alone. I'll see him at home."
>
> When Mom got to the airport, my brother was mad. "Why didn't you let Cara pick me up?" He was irritable and silent on the drive home.
>
> Mom dropped him at my house and didn't say a word. She was actually mad at *me* about it. I saw her look of sadness as she

drove off. Once again, her expectations were disappointed. She wanted to have this car full of love, and I felt I'd let her down. The next day she still wouldn't talk about it, but I know she was sad. She always seems mad at me. I wish we could talk honestly.

What moms often don't realize in the midst of their own sad feelings is that their daughters often feel bad about the disconnect too, even if they've surrounded themselves with a tough shell.

Sometimes there's a lot you want to know about your daughter's life, but she now tells her roommate or husband the things she used to talk about with you when she lived at home. Although it can hurt, there are reasons daughters avoid talking about certain subjects with their mothers. Part of letting her mature is accepting that she doesn't want Mom to know about every area of her life.

Another reason our daughters don't tell us everything is that they expect disapproval or anticipate that we may become fearful when they reveal a problem. For example, thirty-two-year-old Annamarie told me, "My mom's one of my best friends, but I know what to tell her and what not to tell her. I don't have full disclosure with her. She lives two hours away and is in a constant state of fear about everything. If I have bad news, I don't tell her until there's a resolution or I have a plan to solve the problem. When my two-year-old daughter was going through blood tests, I didn't share it with her. I don't want to give her anything else to worry about. I often feel like I'm trying to protect her."

We all do this at times; I did with my mother because she was quite anxious about me and my kids. I would call to ask her to pray if our son had an asthma attack, but I didn't want to overload her with bigger burdens—like telling her when our marriage was strained or I was struggling with insomnia. After all, she had five other grown children and twenty-two grandkids to worry about.

Research shows this tendency is common in daughters. In one study, one-fourth of the women who had a living parent had *never* discussed their marital situation with their moms, "typically because they expected disapproval or lack of understanding." One woman in the study said, "I am ashamed to say it, but at fifty I am still afraid of what my mother thinks…she intimidates me. I was divorced almost a year before I told her."[2]

Instead of overreacting or disapproving, what if we take in stride a misfortune or stressful situation our daughter describes? It's not easy to stay calm. But if we deal with our concerns by letting go of our desire to go into control/fix mode and place the issue in God's hands, our confidence will grow so that with his help, she can figure things out. She's more likely to confide in us next time if our response is calm. After struggling with this myself, my mantra has become, "She'll figure it out." And she always does.

First Peter 5:7 is a great invitation for all our daughter concerns: "Cast all your anxiety on him [God] because he cares for you"—and I would add, he cares for her even more than you and I do. Scriptures like Psalm 55:22 assure us that if we give him our burdens, he will sustain us. Believing these promises, we can live and respond with a healthy degree of peace instead of panic, which is a good role model for our grown daughters to see. We can "cast" or let go of not only the things about our daughter we worry about but our very expectations for the relationship and how much or little we communicate.

LEAVING THE PAST BEHIND

Another major communication buster is bringing up the past. One young woman told me, "My mom always wants to talk about when I was young and about how wonderful those times were when we were all at home.

She sees the old me, not the person I've become. I'm twenty-eight years old now, not twelve or sixteen. I want her to relate to me in the *present*."

Another daughter said, "I don't have a relationship with my mom, and whatever communication we have tends to escalate. Inevitably, our conversation explodes into a fight. She'll bring up the past as if it just happened. Dredging things up and blaming me for situations that happened years ago hurts me. The message I get is that I'm not a good-enough daughter, and there's no forgiveness from her."

This was not expressed by a daughter on the skids but by an outstanding young woman. She feels her mother knows nothing about her life for the last ten years because her mom focuses on the past, doesn't ask, and hasn't sought to know who her daughter is *now*. Her mom doesn't know where her career is going or what she's passionate about in the present. When a mother's interaction with her daughter is based mostly on the past, it may be because her own life is devoid of love and personal fulfillment. So she tries to fill the emptiness with memories of the sweet bygone days when her daughter was home.

Sometimes we mothers dwell on the negatives of the past or react with blaming because our life is in turmoil. If we've not resolved the hurts in our past, we may carry resentment, even if the hurt had nothing to do with our daughter. If we don't have the emotional tools to talk about problems in a healthy way, we may say things that bring more frustration into the relationship. Resolving and letting go of the past, forgiving, and living one day at a time will go a long way in fostering a good relationship with our daughters. Then we are less likely to get stuck in the "old times."

I know what it's like to have some baggage from the past or to feel regret about what I didn't do right. But meeting with a skilled counselor has helped me resolve those issues and rediscover the joy of living in the present. When our focus is on living well *today* instead of dwelling on what happened in all the yesterdays, we'll move forward. We may even become more interesting, enjoyable people our daughters might actually like spending time with.

SHARING OUR FLAWS

It greatly benefits our communication when we're transparent about our humanity. Like me, you probably put your heart and soul into mothering and want the best for your children. Yet as mothers, we are fallible human beings who make mistakes and fail in spite of our best intentions. Sometimes that leads us to be defensive or try to appear as the noble mother who is right and not reveal our own flaws *because we're the mom.* This pretense doesn't draw our daughters to us. Daughters usually know their moms' flaws full well; we aren't hiding anything from them. It takes humility to admit them, but that very honesty is a marvelous bridge-builder in the relationship.

You see, our daughters aren't interested in the pretense of the perfect woman. Instead, they value honesty and transparency. Our real influence comes when we're open with them about our failures, but they see how we're overcoming them. So as my counselor, Ruthie, says, "Let them see you as the fallen critters that you are!"

We all have foibles and quirks regarding how we relate to others. Some of these are personality-based and some are from our family of origin. For example, some families have a mean or sarcastic streak that impedes good communication. Others have misplaced humor and target one or two family members for snide comments that derail honest communication—then say, "I was just kidding!" afterward. Or they become defensive or rationalize if anyone speaks truth about their behavior or how they've been hurt.

I've struggled with a tendency to explain and defend my actions if Ali or someone else criticizes me. Growing up I heard others in my family do this, so I followed the pattern. But when I realized this was a roadblock in conversations with Ali (as well as others), I decided to fess up to it. After all, once we see a roadblock in the relationship, we don't have to perpetuate it. A few days after my self-observation, Ali and I sat across from each other drinking a latte. When I shared about my realization, she was relieved because it was out in the open. Then we were free to move forward.

Another foible I'm working on is taking things personally. I'm sensitive by nature (called "hypersensitive" as a child) so my feelings are easily hurt. The problem is when I take things personally, I'm not really open to what my daughter is saying, and she isn't totally honest because she's protecting my feelings. I've asked God to help me on this, and he is giving me some really good opportunities to practice not taking things personally. As I do, I'm reminded that what someone says or does may be more about what she is feeling at the time than it is about me, and I just need to let it go and listen.

Another pattern that really pushes a daughter's buttons is for her mom to give input and advice on things she's been doing for herself and doesn't need Mom's help with. It might be cooking ("Honey, this would be a much better way to slice the tomato"), laundry ("You know, you really shouldn't put those colors together." "But I'm thirty-eight—why are you telling me this? I've been washing my own clothes for years!"), parenting, or household matters. Your input—when unrequested—is insulting because it makes her feel like a kid. It's much better to teach by example and keep your "two cents" to yourself unless she asks for it.

If any of these foibles ring true or others come to your mind, talk with your daughter about them and ask God to make you more aware of when they slip into your conversation so you can back up and apologize to your daughter.

I don't mean to imply that all conversation snafus are our fault, moms. Sometimes the responsibility lies with our daughters. But I have learned that *awareness of my part* if there is a misunderstanding or conflict is half the battle. Being willing to look at this has really helped Ali and my communication.

LISTENING ATTENTIVELY

The kind of conversations that enrich and encourage, comfort and challenge, begin with a listening heart. It's a gift when we have moments to truly connect with our daughters, to share real feelings and experiences. But to connect like this we need to become better listeners.

Here's what a thirty-something who is struggling in her marriage and swamped with caring for three young children shared with me. "I'm the opposite of my friends who want space from their moms and don't want them to interfere in their lives. I've asked my mom to sit down and *talk with me and listen to me,* but she isn't listening. She wants to buy me turkey or grapes or race by my house and do the dishes before she races out. I want her to emotionally connect with me, and I wish she would listen. But we end up lashing out or not saying anything."

The daughter continued. "Mom says, 'I'm here for you,' but it doesn't match her actions. When we have a conflict, she never admits her mistakes and tries to act like everything's okay. I wish she could deal with reality and not distance herself from me when we have problems."

Do you hear the longing? The desire this daughter has for her mom to emotionally engage in conversation instead of distancing, to deal with reality, and admit her mistakes? And most of all, she would love to be listened to. Her mom genuinely may be trying to help by doing the pile of dishes or bringing fruit. But her daughter doesn't want *things or service* as much as she *desires connection.* Sometimes moms do this because they don't know how to be intimate; it's too scary to get close. Or perhaps this mother is overwhelmed by the thought that her daughter is struggling and she doesn't know how to help. But the point is, she doesn't have to *do anything*. Just listen.

Sometimes without realizing it, I too have "bought turkey and grapes"—doing what I thought would help instead of sitting down and asking or emotionally connecting with my daughter. Have you? I've found that listening well to what our daughters really *need* rather than responding out of what *we want to give* goes a long way to building bridges of understanding.

Could you identify with any of the situations in this chapter? If you've ever had misunderstandings or frustrating conversations, let me encourage you to become a more active listener.

"Active listening," therapist Ruthie Hast explains, "involves us in *introspection, reflection,* and ultimately, *restoration.*"[3] Isn't that what we're hoping for—restoration of our relationship?

Though I'm still working on this, I've found that being an attentive listener means the world to Ali. Daughters want to feel heard, and active listening is a great way to facilitate that. If you apply the following active listening principles to your mother-daughter conversations, it can work wonders:

First, when she's speaking, give her time to say what she needs to say and *avoid interrupting*. Avoid finishing her sentences; it really shuts daughters down, especially if they're quiet by nature. This is a tough one for those of us who think we know what they're going to say next, but you can do it!

Next, make a conscious effort to hear not only her words but the *total message* she's sending. Then summarize in a few words what you heard before you jump in and react or change the subject. This not only communicates respect and interest, it encourages her to talk, cry, say whatever she needs to express, and know you are a safe place. You're tuned in to her.

Focus on *understanding* her and her message rather than giving pat answers or advising—or telling her why she's wrong. It's worth the effort because when we're actively listening, we can discern why she sees or acts in a situation differently than we would. As we come to better understand her, it leads ultimately to forgiveness and communicates grace, which are key "notes" in the mother-daughter duet.

• A Daughter's Perspective •

In communication, one of my greatest needs is to feel heard—up-and-down feelings and all. As daughters, we want to be heard, not as just our mothers' children, but as equals, as adults. We want to be one of two women talking and listening back and forth like old friends. Nowadays that's sometimes how Mom and I relate.

During election time, I loved bantering back and forth with her about political issues. I love debating and hearing her views and telling her mine. We shared stories and editorial comments we'd heard on television or radio news programs. But sometimes when I'm with my mother, I don't want to talk at all. I just want my space.

So do many women I know. We want our moms to understand that pushing us to talk will usually drive us away from you. But we really love it when you genuinely want to listen and don't have any expectations for our answers. We need you to know that we are in the process of finding our voice and separating our vocals (so to speak) from your vocals—because part of being an adult is finding our own voice. If we don't talk to you the way you want us to, perhaps we need space and time to figure out our language that is different than yours. We could end up creating a lovely, interesting harmony once found.

We want you to know that we are thinking, feeling, unique individuals. And part of *becoming* our own woman is finding out how we sound to the rest of the world, working out our communication quirks so we can relate to people other than mother, father, sister, and brother. We hope you'll give us some space and time while we get there!

My mom and I have learned in recent years how to be open about ways we communicate that are counterproductive. We go head to head on some issues, but we think of it as healthy now. I think it's necessary to continually accept our differences in thoughts and feelings. She's come a long way in being a good listener. And I hope I'm becoming a better listener without giving her advice! I love to talk with Mom over coffee at Starbucks these days, sharing ideas or an NPR story I've heard.

But this has been a definite process—full of forgiveness, practice, empathy, and taking responsibility for our own emotions during conversation. It's been a process of unlearning communication habits that most certainly didn't work and both of us being open to new ways of relating. We've learned these through taking breaks from each other, mother-daughter counseling, and lots of trying, failing, and then trying again. I've learned through the hard relational work we've done that I'd rather spend more energy on the positive aspects of my mom than focus on the negative. Life is too short to stay resentful and annoyed. I hope the same revelation is true for her.

Two-Part Harmony

The important thing, Ann Caron says in *Mothers to Daughters,* is to keep communicating. "When mothers and daughters stop talking and do not attempt to understand their differences, they create an emotional distancing that is disabling to each. If they are able to argue through their conflicts and still love each other, they keep emotionally connected. The impassioned give-and-take, the interruptions, the emotional upheavals will not harm mothers and daughters as long as they keep talking and listening to each other."[4]

Remember, when your daughter is not into having deep conversations with you, it helps to realize that right now she might need to find answers and advice outside of you. Marge and her daughter had a good relationship, but in adulthood, her daughter sought mentors beyond her mom. They still relate; she baby-sits her grandkids and they see each other regularly. But the in-depth conversations just aren't there for now. Though this has been painful at times, it's been something Marge has accepted. Like this mom, you and your daughter might have had great communication in junior high school and then it got progressively worse as she got closer to leaving home. And you're left hurting and wondering, "I need her still; doesn't she need me? I love to talk to my daughter and I miss her companionship. Doesn't she need my opinions, my help, my advice?"

Think of communicating with your daughter as an ongoing, sometimes rocky road, full of ebb and flow. But along the way, you'll have wonderful times of connection, finding out who your adult daughter truly is and is becoming. Remember—don't try so hard, enjoy the process, listen well, give space and grace, enjoy talks with your girlfriends when your daughter seems silent, and know that daughters still appreciate you even when they don't affirm your words. Love consists of much more than words. Sometimes things like silence and hugs and acceptance can communicate the most.

Look for opportunities that foster moments together just *being*. No expectations, just fun moments together. We offer a number of creative ideas for connecting in the next chapter that you might want to try. Then see what happens—without an agenda you could just be surprised. Maybe, just maybe, she *does* want to talk.

If you're ready to listen.

CONNECTING
AND BONDING

⬤ ⬤ ⬤ ⬤ ⬤

I learned to love the journey, not the destination. I
learned that this is not a dress rehearsal, and that
today is the only guarantee you get.

—ANNA QUINDLEN, QUOTED IN *THE LIVES OUR MOTHERS LEAVE US*

⬤ ⬤ ⬤ ⬤ ⬤

ackpacks hanging on our shoulders, Ali, Maggie (who is now
my daughter-in-law), and I rolled our small black suitcases
through the crowded Paris train station. The three of us had traveled
through England, France, Germany, Switzerland, and Italy and now were
on the last leg of our eighteen-day journey. Little did I know how much
good this trip would do our mother-daughter relationship.

With our college-student budget, we rode trains to get to each destination. We encountered the usual travel glitches but had fun overcoming them together. Our journey included surviving one of the worst heat
waves in Europe's history, getting lost in a huge city, and being assigned
to a sleeping car on a night train with five pot-smoking German guys. We
shared cheese crackers, PMS, and many espressos. Along the way, I got to
know Maggie before she married our son and got to know Ali better in a
different context than we'd ever had.

On the high-speed train to London to catch our flight home, Ali and I were mistakenly assigned to a different car than Maggie. It ended up being our most bonding moment on the trip.

As the train sped along, a tuxedo-clad waiter came to our table and set sparkling ice water and a delicious appetizer on the crisp linen table-cloth. He followed that with Salade Niçoise. We shared a luncheon of scallops, asparagus and peas in tarragon cream. No one hurried us, and we talked and talked, lingering over our food. Our attentive waiter refilled our glasses and scraped the crumbs off the table with a knife into a napkin before serving the *pièce de résistance* — chocolate mousse and butter *gallettes* served with a dark roast coffee and cream. This was the best food we'd had in weeks.

Though our lunch was great, the conversation was even better. Up to this point there had been the normal tension or a few sharp words preceded by, "Oh Mom!" during the trip. But in those moments in the dining car, everything was forgotten. We laughed and talked about the funny incidents along the way. For the first time in a long time, our conversation harmonized instead of clashing.

Suddenly my daughter looked me in the eye and said words I'll never forget. "Mom, I didn't realize *how fun you are,* how spontaneous you are! I just hadn't thought you were a fun person for such a long time. But you are!"

That comment from Ali made the whole trip worthwhile.

Months of tension dissolved in the moments together. An added benefit of the trip was that I stopped relating to Alison as my youngest child and began admiring some new strengths. She could figure out any big-city subway system, exchange different currencies, and speak to French people as though she were a native. Since French isn't my forte and I'm directionally challenged, I was immensely grateful for Ali's great sense of direction and her ability to order at French restaurants with ease. I was struck by how her flexibility made travel less stressful for her. She didn't get upset about a change of plans or have a lot of expectations to fulfill. She just enjoyed the moments and what she discovered along the way. She actually seemed to come alive "on the road." Had we never traveled together, I might not ever have grown to appreciate and affirm some of these wonderful qualities.

CLIMBING THE HEIGHTS TOGETHER

For Alice, a woman I met from upstate New York, and her daughter, a Rocky Mountain hiking trip proved the best bonding experience they'd ever had. Caroline had just dropped out of a pre-nursing major and was directionless. She'd broken up with her boyfriend and was feeling down. Alice and her daughter lived in different states and had only spent time together when the whole family gathered for the crazy, busy activities of the holidays with little time for one-on-one talk. But on their trip, it was just mother and daughter, and they had a chance to reconnect. They hiked during the day, sometimes stopping for a picnic on the trail. At night they grilled out and slept in a cozy cabin.

As the week unfolded, through watching stunning sunsets and sharing simple meals and steaming mugs of green tea, their communication flowed. They found a new harmony and closeness in their relationship as Caroline opened up about her fears and dreams. Alice could listen without any interruptions. After the trip, Caroline went back to college with new enthusiasm to face the uncertainties. With their friendship renewed, Alice and her daughter kept in touch. Not the superficial conversations they used to have—"How are you, Mom?" "Fine, a little busy. How's school?"—but about things that really mattered to them.

MOTHER-DAUGHTER BONDING

You don't have to go far away or spend five days to have some good mother-daughter connection time. Though being away from the busyness of home can help you reconnect, you could feel "away" at a café that serves high tea or take an afternoon outing on a bike path in your city.

While in Washington DC last year, I met a mother and her two adult daughters having high tea at the Ritz-Carlton. This was a fancy, lovely environment—the special tearoom with tapestry settees, classical music in the background, and the most delicious selection of teas, cakes, and strawberries with whipped cream you've ever tasted. A few times a year this mom and her daughters, who each live in a different city, meet at this midpoint hotel specifically to enjoy tea and a few relaxed hours of conversation. It helps them stay connected though all three have demanding careers.

Connection time might mean a shopping expedition. If your daughter enjoys shopping, that might be a vehicle for you to bond. Looking for shoes or designer bags at a special price, perusing antique furniture shops or flea markets, or just window shopping at your local mall can afford a fun experience if this is your bent.

A Daughter's Perspective

I'm not going to lie. Some of my favorite bonding times with my mom are when she takes me to coffee or lunch and picks up the tab. Or when we go to a movie and she springs for my ticket. Or when she takes me shopping for my birthday and buys me a new shirt. It probably sounds selfish to enjoy time with her when she treats me to something. But as an adult, it really is a way that I feel loved. It happens to be one of my love languages. Because gift giving is something I thoroughly enjoy doing for others, I feel loved and cared for when my mom speaks the language back. It's not so much about how much money is spent; it's about feeling special for that little bit of time. The same applies to when she offers to take me out to do something I really enjoy.

For me, it's a cup of coffee and great conversation about politics or philosophy, in an "open mind" kind of conversation that helps me feel bonded and close. It's the simple things in the midst of the busyness of life, like dinner at an ambient restaurant, unrushed and unplanned. Or when in the middle of the day if I have a baby-sitter or the boys are at a friend's house, my mom will agree on a whim to go to a movie with me and "seize the moment." These are ways that I have felt close to my mom in the past, even when we've been at odds. These are still the ways I connect with her most.

We've always enjoyed getting out of town together, away from the norm or the stress. We have in common the sheer enjoyment of travel and spontaneity. With all the things we differ on, from personality to preference of music, we share a sense of adventure. She's encouraged that sense of adventure in me through the years with her "go for it" attitude about my desire to travel and see the world.

Even when we don't have the resources to travel as much as we would like, there have been some very practical, real ways that I've felt a connection to my mom through doing simple things together.

A more "post age thirty" way we've connected is by meeting up at a café and sitting without an agenda and chatting over current issues in government or the education system, or I tell her things I'm learning from my wonderful boys, Noah and Luke. Our topics of conversation used to be fraught with too much struggle to find common ground to endure a coffee date. I wanted the ease of this scenario for years before it became reality. But when it did and we began taking a half hour here or there to chat at a familiar café, I felt as if my mom really was seeing what would help me feel closer to her, what my version of fun is. I felt like she became willing and able to get on my turf.

Then I tend to open up more and feel safe that we aren't meeting for a covert daughter-improvement moment. I love to see her enjoying herself, removing herself from rote activity and willing to have some fun. It means the world to me. The real breakthrough when I felt truly safe and bonded with her was when we would meet and sit at an outdoor café during my smoking days. I openly would enjoy a cigarette, and she had gotten over the fact that I smoked, and she didn't judge me anymore. She sat there and enjoyed our time as if it was the most normal thing in the world. I know she didn't want me to smoke because of obvious health risks, but she didn't harp, she didn't show worry; she simply sat and enjoyed the time we had together. And so did I. Even though I was doing something she felt was unhealthy, I felt acceptance. And later, she willingly helped with the boys when I was going through nicotine withdrawals.

I love going to the movies with my mom too. She's not afraid to go to the indie flicks that I love, and I can appreciate her chick flicks, historical fiction, and romantic comedies. We both enjoy taking a break from reality, and movies are a natural stress reliever for us. I've most enjoyed watching *Parenthood* (a good one to rent annually), *Pride and Prejudice, Sense and Sensibility,* and *The Joy Luck Club* with Mom. We always chat about how we found common ground with the characters or theme.

Another interesting way we've found to connect is taking personality tests and comparing the outcome of each other's tests. As my mom and I did a free one online, we realized mom was 100 percent extroverted and I was 100 percent introverted, but we were both idealists and feelers. Wow, it was quite a lot of insight. Plus it was really fun to talk all the results out, laugh about our obvious differences, and marvel at what we had in common that we never would have realized otherwise.

The test was a really fun, easy way to get extra insight into this most complex relationship. I'm a natural-born analyzer, so understanding my mom in terms of personality helped me see her differently and helped me see ways that I'd judged her unfairly. And why some things bugged me. We laughed about realizing some of our biggest differences—and some similarities.

Besides understanding her personality, daughters love being asked what we like to do and then mothers have to be willing to do it with us. I know one friend who loves when her mom occasionally meets her after work to share a decadent dessert. They had never done anything like that before her mom asked her what she typically enjoyed doing with her friends. Then her mom said she'd like to meet her out at her favorite place sometime. My friend invited her mom to her favorite artsy pub downtown, and her mom took her up on it. They ended up bonding over conversation and happy hour in a way they had never enjoyed before.

As daughters we most of all appreciate moments that are natural and spontaneous and we don't feel under scrutiny. We enjoy and appreciate being taken to get a pedicure with our moms. However, we don't enjoy time together, no matter what we're doing, if we feel scrutinized or judged. That makes us feel distant and less interested in getting together with you the next time. There was a period of time when I avoided any activity with my mom because I felt like she was worrying about me the whole time we hung out. I could sense her wanting to say something or pray something or just plain change me and make me happy, and I became pretty closed to doing a whole lot of mother-daughtering around town.

Most of all, we love it when you're real with us, when you relate stories of your life and are enjoying yourself when we go places together. If we're honest, we love when you pick up the tab, but we love being able to afford buying you an outfit or a cup of coffee, too, if you'll let us. It means a lot when you are open to an activity that might be new to you, and that helps us to be open to your ideas as well. Please forgive us when we turn you down, be patient with us when we don't want to talk, and don't give up hope that we'll find a way we both enjoy connecting and providing in each other a place to find common ground and stress relief.

Fresh Idea: TAKE A PERSONALITY OR TEMPERAMENT TEST

Personality types can help us understand the ways we relate to situations and people. Consider inviting your daughter to take a personality test when you do and then discussing what you've discovered. This can be a great way to learn something about yourself and about your daughter. The insights you gain could change the way you relate to each other, help you make sense of her job or relationship choices, or just make better sense of *who she is*. If you're open, you can always learn something new about someone—even if you've known each other a long time. To find a personality test, Google "personality tests," or check out www.testcafe.com.

Two-Part Harmony

While there's no magic formula for bonding, resolving conflicts, or reconnecting, we've found there's nothing more healing than having fun together as mom and daughter. As Dr. Ruth Nemzoff says in *Don't Bite Your Tongue: How to Foster Rewarding Relationships with Your Adult Children,* "One can communicate in many ways, and talking is only one of them.

Sometimes we use words. Sometimes a bike ride or a shopping trip serves to cement bonds or to recall happier times.… You can build a relationship based on mutual interests, just as you would with a friend. Sharing experiences and bonding over common hobbies is communicating. These intersections make great conversation starters."[1]

You might make an inventory of your daughter's interests and yours and see where they intersect. Doing activities you enjoy together isn't meant as a fix-all, but done in the right spirit, devoid of agenda or heavy expectations, it can be a means to mending and rebonding with each other or simply maintaining your friendship.

Here are some other mother-daughter activities you might consider:

Make your own soundtrack. If you're taking a road trip, make your own mother-daughter CD with each of your favorite tunes to play in the car. Or if asked, your daughter might be willing to download your favorite songs on her iPod. Bring an adapter to create great background music for relaxing and enjoying the ride.

Walk for a cause. Choose a walkathon or a 5K run like the Susan G. Komen Race for the Cure that you and your daughter can train for and/or participate in together (visit ww5.komen.org/findarace.aspx to find the information on your city). This is something you can do together, even if you don't live in the same city. Google what walks and benefit runs are available in your area—or your daughter's—and then choose one that works for both of you. This can be a way to give something worthwhile and to help the two of you bond in the process. You don't have to be an athlete to do this. A friend pushed her mom in a wheelchair for a fund-raising walk for multiple sclerosis. A mother and daughter we know had a tremendous experience training with Team Leukemia and then walked a marathon to raise money for pediatric cancer research. (Visit www.teamintraining.org for athletic events that benefit leukemia, lymphoma and myeloma research.)

List the strengths and weaknesses in your relationship and share them. When you've had tension in your relationship, it's easy to just look at the problems or weaknesses. But when we become aware of the strengths, we create new ways to connect.

When Ali and I did this, we each listed a few weaknesses. But the amazing thing was how many strengths we both saw. Ali noted that I really value her opinions and admire her creativity and the unique way she mothers her boys, that we apologize when we realize we're wrong and forgive each other, and that we're both lifelong learners. I listed that we both love travel, writing, sharing pithy quotations, music, and her precious sons, for example. This turned out very encouraging for both of us. Consider what might be the weaknesses and strengths in your relationship with your daughter. Our sense is that you might be surprised at the strong elements that are already in your connection.

Watch mother-daughter movies. Watching a movie with a mother-daughter theme can make a terrific evening together. Here are some of our favorites to get you started: *The Joy Luck Club, Then She Found Me, Because I Said So, One True Thing, Pride and Prejudice, Becoming Jane, Something's Gotta Give, Steel Magnolias,* and *Real Women Have Curves.* There are lots of others to pick from the recent and distant past, and these shared movie experiences make great conversation starters. If she's up for a chat afterward, a good question to ask after watching is: which character did you most identify with?

If you don't live close, plan a mother-daughter dinner via webcam and Skype. Or maybe you could ask what your daughter's favorite show is and then both watch it every week and talk about it the next day. Reality shows like *American Idol* or *Dancing with the Stars* are great for this because you start feeling like you know the people and you can cheer for your favorites along with your daughter—or debate your individual preferences. Either way, it provides you with common ground, which fosters connection.

Have audio book discussions. Sarah and her married daughter who has three kids choose an audio book to read together each month. They don't have a lot of sit-down time in their schedules for reading, so audio books work great. They take turns choosing the book and each have a copy of it on CD to listen to in their cars during work commute, carpool, or errand times. Listening to the same book at the same time and discussing it periodically has given this mother and daughter terrific common ground for conversations, especially since they take turns picking the book. They've covered a wide range of genres: biographies, historical fiction, English or American novels, memoirs, nonfiction inspirational books, and self-help. But whatever they're reading and discussing, it's been a bonding experience.

Tip from Ali: Make your conversation *about the book*. And avoid self-help unless your daughter loves the book and chooses it on her own. Resist choosing a certain book because you want to teach her something that you think will improve her. Your daughter might lose interest in sharing books with you if she senses your motives are such. Again, if you don't live in the same town, this activity and the next are something you could do over the phone or even over the Internet with a webcam.

Do a book swap. Go to your local bookstore or library together (or if you're in different places, peruse the selections on Amazon.com while you're both on the computer) to pick out a new book. Then after the book hunt, switch books, and you each read the other's. This can open your eyes to a different genre or something outside the box of what you'd ordinarily choose, plus bring some new understanding to your relationship. Then meet up in two weeks at a favorite dinner place or, if living apart, Skype or e-mail, and discuss what you learned about the other's interests, generation, and so on.

Enjoy pedi or mani moments. In the thick of writing this book and the multiple tasks we each had, I called Ali one afternoon and asked her if she could get a baby-sitter for a short while and meet me at a nail salon for a pedicure. This wasn't a regular occurrence for us, but it was relaxing and fun. Sitting next to each other in the big massage spa chairs, we looked at magazines, helped each other choose nail colors, and chatted. For a new twist, pick out the color for each other and agree to go with whatever the other picks. If your daughter favors black nail colors, Mom, you're brave to let her choose yours and actually wear it, but it could be an interesting time together!

Get artsy. If your daughter is artistically inclined, visit an art museum or an artsy movie theater or coffee shop. Get out of any ruts, and just have fun. Or start a new tradition: during the week of Mother's Day, go together to a do-it-yourself pottery place and paint a coffee mug or plate, and then exchange them. There's nothing more therapeutic than quietly doing art together, and you don't have to be a van Gogh to enjoy the experience. The mug or plate may become a treasure and a way to preserve some positive memories.

Have a mother-daughter dinner. Carolyn and her three adult daughters meet once a month at one of their houses for dinner and conversation. Since they rotate homes, the hostess gets to choose the menu and decide on the topic of conversation. When Carolyn was raising her daughters, they didn't dialogue or spend a lot of time together. Mom and Dad worked hard, and they hadn't been role models of good family conversations. So the girls and their mom weren't good friends as adults until they started their mom-daughter evenings. One night, Tanya decided they'd each tell five things they liked about the others. Another evening they talked about some family memories and looked at photos. These evenings together are mending and rebuilding their connections.

Get a makeover. Go makeup shopping together, and if makeovers are available at a department store makeup counter, both of you have one. Ask for your daughter's input on the "look of the moment," and take her advice on some pointers she gives you. She may just be able to help you look a little younger.

Try new restaurants together, once a month or when you can get together instead of going to the same old place. Search out ones with great ambience and food. Try to find out what food your daughter really enjoys—Thai, Indian, Chinese-Vietnamese, and go there.

Learn something new. When Catherine's relationship with her daughter was strained, she asked Elizabeth what she really wanted to learn and explore. Elizabeth loved to cook. So she signed the two of them up for every cooking class she could find. When there, they didn't have to talk about anything negative. They had a delightful three hours of being together, intently watching and learning from the chefs. They had some neutral pleasant conversation but mostly their focus was on the cooking. The cooking classes kept mother and daughter connected during their most difficult communication periods. They kept building bridges. More understanding grew—and they both became excellent gourmet cooks.

All these are ways to experience life together and have time together, and some are meaningful even when there are miles between the two of you. Not just to labor over heavy communication issues and try to resolve, resolve, resolve. But to go to your daughter's turf—sharing in what she enjoys and inviting her to do something you love—and discover why she likes that activity by participating in it yourself. Be direct and simply ask for a movie time or a block of time to do one of the above activities. As you take a vacation from issues using any of these ideas, watch your connection grow.

ARE YOU GOING TO CHURCH, HONEY?

• • • • •

Children aren't coloring books. You don't get to
fill them with your favorite colors.
—KHALED HOSSEINI, *THE KITE RUNNER*

• • • • •

M y mom thinks she's religious because when the church doors
open, she's there, but I think I have more of a personal relationship with God," said one young woman as a group of us talked in a
local café. "Legalism, churchgoing, and appearances are important to her.
I don't worry about what people are thinking about me and my spiritual
life. As long as I'm still pursuing God, whether in church or not, I'm still
connected with him and enjoy our relationship. But my mom doesn't see
it that way, and I'm sad she can't share in my joy."

"Our moms try to guide us in the direction that's familiar to them,"
said another. "They want us to find God earlier to spare us pain, but what
they don't take into account is they got there through hard times. No one
can tell us how to find God. We have to find him on our own," another
daughter said.

"When my dad was in the worst stages of his alcoholism, my mom
turned to God and dove into the Bible," explained a thirty-year-old. "She

got through everything by getting really close with God. She even got a master's degree in theological studies. When my husband had addiction problems last year, she put too much pressure on me to get into the Bible, go to lots of Bible studies, and do it like she did. She took a certain path, and to her, it's the familiar, right way, and there's a wrong way. But I like to take the untrodden path. I've got to have the freedom to find God for myself."

As we've talked with many daughters in their twenties, thirties, and beyond, one theme emerges: they want their own spiritual journey to be respected, not put down or devalued. Many said, "I want my mother to remember her own journey and know I have to have my own journey as well."

Your daughter may be actively relating to a church body and God, or she may be a seeker, even when it doesn't look like it on the outside. Her faith may not look like what we expect. It may appear in ways unfamiliar to us since spirituality is deeply personal and based on their experience—not ours.

She may be part of a movement that is reaching out to social activism, into going green or saving orphans. As Suzanne Eller, who works with hundreds of young adults, says, "They want to change the world, feed the homeless, design a Web site that helps fund a well in Africa." Though they may not be interested in going to church as an obligation, they want to be part of a community that's relevant and makes a difference in the world today.

Young women aren't afraid to wrestle with the tough questions: *What has God created me to do? What purpose am I on earth for? Why? Why? Why? And who is God anyway?* Sometimes it's the questioning and doubting that worries moms the most. As Christian mothers we have a deep desire for our daughters to follow God and love him with all their hearts. We *long* for them to walk in the truth and have prayed for years that they would. We've invested a lot in building a firm foundation since early childhood. We took them to church, had family devotions, and sacrificed to send them to private schools or camp. When our daughters leave home and seem to leave their faith behind, it can be a source of disappointment and anxiety.

THE GREEN STAMP MENTALITY

Therapist Leslie Vernick, author of *How to Find Selfless Joy in a Me-First World,* and I were discussing the disappointment we hear from moms whose adult children have seemed to turn their backs on the beliefs they were raised with. In her counseling practice she sees many women with what she calls the "Green Stamp mentality." A few decades ago, when a woman went to the grocery store and spent a certain amount of money, she was given Green Stamps to stick in a small book. When the book was all filled with stamps, she could redeem it for prizes.

In a similar way, moms today seem to feel they deserve to "redeem" all the hard work they put into raising their daughters.

Women say, "I was a good mom. We were a good family. I took my daughter to a great church, sent her on youth ski trips, and prayed for her. I deserve a better kid!"

Besides being just plan angry at God because he didn't come through with the "prize," moms struggle with feeling guilty that somehow *we* didn't do enough to produce daughters like our friends seem to have. When we're disappointed with how God is handling their lives, that anger causes us to distance ourselves from him, and to question his sovereignty and goodness. That anger erodes our faith and fuels a desire to take over control and "fix" our daughters spiritually. But often at the core of all these emotions, what we feel is *fear.*[1]

When your daughter isn't following the spiritual path you think she should choose, you might be afraid she'll be captured by evil and forever lost. Hearing statistics that a high percentage of people forsake their faith when they leave high school and don't come back in their adulthood causes further anxiety.

But take heart; questioning and doubting is a good thing. In fact, it's entirely normal. And in the long run, it's best to let a daughter sort out her own faith whether she has a spiritual awakening in her twenties, thirties, or not at all. We simply can't micromanage her faith or speed up her spiritual journey anyway. We can, however, gain a larger perspective by understanding what is involved with individuating and becoming an adult when it comes to spirituality. If she's still "in the far country," living with a heart that's away from her Creator in later life, we keep praying for her, but it's not our journey to manage. We may not see her walk in the fullness of Christ in our lifetime, but we can know God will be faithful and has her best interests at heart.

GROWING AN ADULT FAITH

A woman came to Dr. Catherine Hart Weber's office[2] for counseling. "I never did anything bad," she said. "I've always followed the Lord and never questioned. Why does my daughter? *What's wrong with her?*"

"Nothing is wrong with your daughter," Dr. Weber assured her. The Christian therapist explained that part of becoming an adult is sorting through your beliefs and experiences to choose how to integrate them and live them out. And the issue of who questions and who doesn't has more to do with *personality and temperament* than it does with how rebellious or "good" a person is. For example, some women's personalities cause them to be very private about their faith journey, whereas others are very expressive. But just because they aren't sharing about what God's doing in their lives or what they're praying about doesn't mean he isn't working.

The strong, independent personality will tend to test and question everything, including spiritual issues. She needs to find out for herself what she believes and the ideals she wants to live by, not just read somebody else's views in a book or follow her parents. This process may begin in the adolescent years if a young woman is more mature or analytical in her thinking. Or she may begin to wrestle with faith issues in college or years after when she gets married or goes through a crisis of some kind.

The compliant, submissive daughter often tends to follow what she was taught growing up. "I'll do what my parents did; it worked for them" might be her approach—at least for now. This daughter may live the model Christian life in high school and college, yet not have individuated and discovered her own beliefs apart from her mom and dad's.

Some of the people who follow along with a "coattail" faith never question until midlife. Then a situation or crisis pushes them into discovering their own foundation for their passion, beliefs, and values. At that point they may stop going to church, change religions, get divorced from their Christian spouse, embrace one philosophy or another—and moms are left wondering: *What happened?* What's occurring in them may be just a delayed phase of individuating spiritually.

Other daughters, especially those whose parents have high spiritual expectations and control, can maintain a spiritual facade but lead a secret life underneath. She keeps her parents happy by acting like the model good girl on the outside, but inside her faith is empty and stagnant. If she doesn't feel her mom will accept her different beliefs, she simply leaves her parent out of that part of her life. Without the freedom to depart from her parents' way of approaching spirituality, she may become dishonest and develop a hidden life. However, when we give our daughters the freedom to be honest about how they're living and what they're thinking, and we keep putting them in God's hands through prayer, stop being their personal Holy Spirit, and take our hands off, they have room to grow.

No matter what age our daughters are, it helps to gain perspective. They are pilgrims on the journey of life, just as we mothers are. They're growing and discovering their own core beliefs—in their timetable and God's. Isn't that part of the problem? It's often a different timetable than we would choose.

To our daughters, if mom speaks or acts in fear to what looks like a daughter's being "off the beaten path," it appears we're failing to model the very faith we espouse. And if we put off enjoying her until she blossoms spiritually like we've hoped, she feels unaccepted, and we may miss some significant moments with her. It does fill our heart with joy when we see our daughter's faith growing. But if it's not happening, we may need to accept that it may not be her time to bloom yet. If that is the case, let me encourage you—you planted good seeds and the Master Gardener is still at work even in the unseen. He doesn't make mistakes.

I had no idea that my daughter perceived me as anxious when I'd mention how I was praying for her. For a number of years, I led a mothers' prayer group that met in our home. Twelve to eighteen of us moms prayed—in confidentiality—for our college- and career-age sons and daughters for one hour each week. To me, investing this time of asking God's blessing for our grown kids was one of the best gifts I could give my children. A side benefit was the reduced stress we felt after we'd given God our burdens and requests for our children.

I've recently had an "aha" moment. Ali has a different spiritual language than I do. She doesn't like to talk openly about what the Spirit is doing or what someone prays for her. It's very personal and private to her. (She's very much like her dad in that quality.) The disconnect was that I assumed she'd be like me.

The problem was I thought that knowing Mom was praying for her would be a blessing to her as it was to me. You see, when my mom was alive and called to say she was praying for me and my family, I was grateful. We lived several hundred miles apart, and in a medical crisis or other problem, it was comforting to know she was praying. Though Mom passed away over twenty-five years ago, it still blesses me to know somebody cares enough to pray. But not my daughter! It made her feel there was something so wrong with her only God could fix it, and did just the opposite of warming her heart.

It was a breakthrough when we talked about our differences on this a year ago. I understood that she resented feeling like my "prayer project." She and many other adult daughters like their privacy and don't want their moms sharing their problems or concerns with *anyone else,* even their prayer group. Understanding our different approaches to spirituality has really boosted our connection.

GET A GRIP ON FEAR

Because we're mothers, we think it's our job to not only be concerned but to worry about our daughters' spiritual life or lack of one. And if they're not doing "well" by our standards, to remediate it. Yet if they sense continual fear in us, they will withdraw and tend to hide things from us.

I know it's extremely difficult not to be anxious when a beloved daughter is going in the opposite direction that you feel and the Bible says leads to life. Maybe you pictured her teaching Sunday school or marrying a pastor. But she tells you she wants to go to India and sit under a tree to find herself, that she's a Zen Buddhist, or perhaps shows no interest in God or traditional church at all. When you hear that, your heart aches.

That heartache comes from the fact that if we've committed our lives to Christ and dedicated this child to God, we moms feel *it's our responsibility* to do all we can to lead her to Christ. And we do, all through their growing-up years. But if our deepest mission and goal is that our daughter walks in the truth (2 John 4), and she is not doing that in the way we think she should, anxiety arises. *Is my daughter saved? Is she on a path of destruction? Will she ever come back to church?* And if the mission isn't accomplished yet, we can feel justified in interfering or giving lectures about what she ought to be doing—even throughout her whole adult life.

When all our daughter perceives in us is anxiety or control, we're not demonstrating the very peace and faith we talk so much about. I was struck by what Wayne Jacobsen, author of *He Loves Me! Learning to Live in the Father's Affection,* said about finding our own security in God's love and our awareness of his unlimited patience with us and how this will redefine the other relationships in our lives. He goes on to explain:

> Instead of demanding that others conform to what you think is right, you will find yourself letting others have their own journey. By no longer manipulating them to what you think is best you can allow them the same freedom God gives you. You will let them choose their own course based on nothing but the clarity of truth as they understand it and the willingness of their conscience. It is the task of the Holy Spirit to convict, not yours.[3]

To overcome this fear, we need to face the fact that *our fear is not faith;* it is not demonstrating faith in God. We need to let go of our fear. But sometimes this kind of letting go is the most excruciating thing a mother can do when she's very concerned about her daughter, as my friend Anna expresses below:

"I was desperate for God to do something to save my daughter's life. She no longer attended church, and she refused to talk with me about her spiritual state. Worse, she had been dangerously using drugs and alcohol for at least two years and had recently become pregnant by a young man she didn't even know. I had attempted everything from prayer to extreme attempts at controlling her behavior. I did it all in love, or so I thought, and I didn't realize that most of my turmoil was rooted in fear. I thought I trusted God. I knew how to stand on his Word. So when I went forward for prayer and counsel at a women's retreat, I expected God to intervene, rescue my daughter, and 'work all things together for good.' I did not expect that he would first rescue me from myself.

"I poured my heart out to one of the counselors, confessing guilt and grief over my perceived failure to save my daughter from certain destruction. Finally, the counselor looked me in the eye and said, 'Honey, you're just not that powerful. You can't control this.' I was stunned and relieved at the same time. I stayed at the altar and continued to pray, this time asking God to forgive me for trying to control it all. While I was on my knees, the Holy Spirit spoke to my heart. *Trust me. I love your daughter even more than you do. And if you died today, I would see to it that she ends up in my kingdom for eternity. It will be in her timing and mine, not yours.*

"Peace wrapped itself around me like a warm blanket as I envisioned my daughter in heaven with God. Suddenly, it didn't matter when or how she would 'get there,' it just mattered that God would never give up on her. I let go of so much fear that day. Faithful to his word, God did intervene and rescue my daughter within the following year. Today, he continues to work all things together for good in her life—and in my relationship with her."

THE VALUE OF RECALLING OUR JOURNEY

When Ali had seen a scandal tear apart our home church in her adolescence and then felt burned by another one, I saw how it hurt her faith, and I felt heartsick about it. *Would she ever want to commit to a church fellowship again? Would she stay angry about what was done, and would that affect her view of God?* I knew that for many people, whether young or old, when they see people in the church being abusive or mean and unloving, they think "If that's how Christians act, I'm not interested in being part of church at all."

Every one of us moms have a different journey toward trusting God with our daughters' eternal destiny and earthly journey. My older sons broke me in well to the fact that it's God's business, not mine, to lead them and that I can trust him. I've come to embrace Ali's and Hans's choices regarding church and their spirituality. I'm not the author of my daughter's faith, and I'm not the finisher either.

And most of all, I believe God is able to transmit his love to her in ways I might never be able to figure out. I've loved seeing him do that. After all, if it's true what Ephesians 3:20 says and I believe that God does more than we could ask or imagine, then he is well able to guide my daughter's heart.

I believe this because I've seen him do it in my own life. When I struggled with Ali's disinterest in church, I recalled my personal experience of finding God—or his finding me. It always helps me let my grown children be themselves and own their own spiritual journey without my interference. My faith journey was along a winding, zigzag path that certainly didn't proceed according to my mom's timetable. My teens and twenties were marked by many questions that weren't answered by Sunday sermons. I'd suffered some devastating losses, and these were experiences that caused me to mistrust God and wonder if he loved me or heard my prayers at all. Thus, I wasn't in a close, connected relationship with him but in a spiritual fog.

My father's early death, my mother's remarriage, my best friend's accidental death, and changes like my big sisters leaving prematurely all shook my sense of security and left my faith in shambles. No one would have known it, but inside I was wrestling and seeking in my own way. In graduate school, I didn't attend Bible studies but read philosophers and theologians, longing to find meaning in life—longing to reconnect with God.

It wasn't until I was almost thirty years old, after seven years of marriage, expecting our third child—Ali—and having experienced some major trials of my own, that I started reading the New Testament for myself. Not as a result of a Bible study or a sermon or a mother's nagging, which fortunately she didn't do. Instead, it was through reading the pages of Matthew, Mark, Luke, and John that the lights came on for me, that I had a life-changing encounter with Jesus Christ and spiritual transformation began.

Because my reconnection with God didn't have anything to do with church but everything to do with grace, that helps me know God isn't limited to working only within the walls of an institution or specific denomination. He's immensely creative with how he reaches out to his children to draw them into relationship.

For Ali, God's grace came through a wise chaplain and a counselor in treatment and the truths of the Twelve Steps of Alcoholics Anonymous, as she'll describe below. As her journey has proceeded, it's helped me to remember how patient God was with me so I can accept her where she is and give her space and grace to grow.

If you or your daughter didn't take a quick, straight path to spiritual maturity, you're not alone. Catherine Hart Weber's journey took twists and turns as well. Her father was a great psychologist; her parents living godly, committed lives. She was told she was *just like her father,* the boy he never had, destined to follow his footsteps and become a noted Christian psychologist. But she would have none of that plan. At nineteen, this strong-willed, intelligent daughter went off to college to study music and art. She got heavily into wellness and nutrition and wanted to help people improve their health.

Most of all, she wanted to go on her *own journey.* Since her parents didn't support her change in direction, she left home, supporting herself with a full-time job while she attended full-time university classes. She tried drugs, experimented and partied, and since the people she hung out with didn't go to church, she didn't either for a while.

Her parents panicked. But she was bent on discovering her own gifts and talents and exploring what God was doing in *her life.* And she did—today Catherine is a superb counselor with a PhD in psychology and a committed follower of Christ. Because of her own experience, she is not worried about her daughters' spiritual lives because ultimately, Catherine doesn't have control over it any more than her parents' did over hers. She endeavors to be more of a mentor and coach to her nineteen- and twenty-four-year-old daughters—not to guilt them into going to church or Bible study.

INSIDE THE SPIRITUAL INFLUENCE BOX

We've shared in this chapter some things *not to do* regarding your daughter and her faith walk—such as not to have unrealistic expectations or lecture or try to control it. One positive thing you can do is to open the door to discussion about spiritual issues by reading books that have influenced your daughter spiritually—and do this with an open heart. Reading something that matters to her gives you a little common ground and can bring more acceptance and understanding about where she is. The benefit is that accepting where she is puts you *inside the influence box* (instead of outside), and she begins to see you as a safe place she might come someday for discussion about her beliefs or values.

Pastor Roc Bottomly from Oklahoma City says it also helps to communicate something like this: "Since you're an adult, I know you're thinking for yourself. I had lots of questions about what's truth and what I believed, and it's normal. If and when I could ever be helpful as a sounding board for you, let me know." That gives your daughter permission to tell you where she is and what she believes *when she's ready*—so plan to wait until that point rather than forcing the issue by bringing up spiritual issues again and again.

In the meantime, show confidence instead of hounding, nagging, or labeling her. Trust me, a daughter doesn't like being labeled "my prodigal," even if she is acting like one. Demonstrate calmness instead of shock if she tells you about practices that are foreign to you. Keep the connection going even if she's almost forty and still doesn't go to church because she's married to an agnostic and lives across the country. If we try to chase our daughters into God things, resentment builds, which jeopardizes the relationship and doesn't advance their movement toward Christ.

For example, one day a counselor met with a mom and her twenty-two-year-old daughter, Sharon, who lived at home while attending a local university.

"What's the problem you're here to discuss?" the counselor asked.

"My daughter is rebelling against us. She isn't getting up and having her quiet time like we do, and she doesn't go to a Bible study or our church anymore. She sometimes meets with some young people in her friend's apartment on Sundays. And that's just not right. It's not the same as church. I need you to help us bring her to her senses," Joyce pleaded.

She hardly let Sharon put a word in as she continued with what she "should do" and "ought to do if she wants the abundant life."

The counselor explained that Joyce has given her daughter building blocks of faith—just as we might give a child a car made of Lego blocks. When she matures she begins to question, "What will happen if I take it apart?" She puts it back together with the same blocks but makes something entirely different—a shape that's entirely hers. As our chapter opening suggests, our kids aren't coloring books, and we don't get to fill in the colors, especially in regard to their spiritual life. It's the normal task of adolescents and adults to individuate their own faith, to choose their own shape and colors of spirituality. But this mom had enjoyed such control she never let her daughter do that. Now Sharon was rejecting all her parents' religious forms.

• *A Daughter's Perspective* •

I was brought up in a faith-filled home. It was full of love and Bible stories. We went to church together, learned Bible verses, and prayed together. My brothers and I saw our parents value and live essential elements of a life of faith, such as respect, hard work, and compassion. I was baptized at age eight; I enjoyed church and the activities within it—up to a point. I feel privileged that I had a family and community that loved and supported one another. We all need that. As a child it provided stability. I'm thankful for every moment my parents shared and lived their faith. I felt like I could fit into that comfy couch of parent/God relationship until I realized I had my own mind, my own body, my own soul.

In high school I began to internalize a lot of questions and qualms I had with "the church." I wanted to believe that everything I grew up with was true, but at the same time, nothing seemed like mine—just "theirs." Doubts turned into ambivalence, and ambivalence was fueled by frustration with seeing hypocrisy and scandal in our church. And feeling judged and pigeonholed by the same institution I grew up in—talked about or shunned by friends when I didn't go to church.

As I got older, what I thought about God somehow got intermingled with skepticism I'd developed from being around cheating preachers, pompous evangelicals, close-minded traditionalists, and what I deemed the opposite of love and acceptance. My developing worldview and philosophies didn't line up with a lot of what I'd been taught in church. I saw formulas for faith as fake and insincere. I struggled to make sense of it and felt like I was even put outside of friendships for searching to make sense of it all, raising the questions to find the God of *my* understanding.

Instead of communicating about the process of my spirituality and questions concerning the church, I hated, blamed, acted out, and judged. This has been the process of many, not all, but many women I know. We have questioned, we have left, we have hated, we have embraced many aspects of faith and religion. Whatever we have done about our own faith, however, we have felt much and pondered much. If we have left the faith or the expression of that faith that you brought us up in, it isn't a personal affront to you. We don't want you to take our wanderings personally.

We need to feel loved and respected by you no matter what we think or believe and however we choose to express it, because ultimately it will change over time. From one experience in life that draws us closer to God and others that lead to us running away from him, they are *our* experiences and part of that sacred journey we're on.

To many of us, God is found in experiencing real life, in art and music, in nature, in mistakes, and in anything that moves us or makes us feel more alive. We don't necessarily find God by studying concepts within church walls or taking part in church-organized outreach. In fact we might "feel" him more outside the church than in it, and many daughters I've talked to sense this feeling has worried you or caused you some distress about our spiritual lives. The spiritual issue with us is one of inclusive ideas, methods, and teachings to mold into what we call our spirituality at different stages.

Thus, our spirituality is transient, moldable, sacred to us, and at times inexpressible. In our adulthood, it's not something we appreciate being dictated to, pushed to talk about, or simplified to one denomination or theology. Perhaps we don't mention or create commentary about our spirituality at all. Maybe we are in a place where we don't want you to impose any more of your faith or the expression of it onto us. Maybe we want to figure it out for ourselves.

My mom has been open to talking with me and not judging where I am spiritually.

I represent a lot of daughters who express faith entirely differently than our mothers. Perhaps we claim to have no faith. Will you love and accept us in that place? Or will you feel compelled to try to evangelize us back into what we grew up with? There are no easy answers or thoughts to consider on this subject. But it's a great subject to have dialogue and open debate about—without an agenda, without trying to change each other.

My friend Lilly has been judged harshly by her mom for her stance on church attendance. The first thing her mom asks when they talk on the phone is if the boys have been to Sunday school yet. Lilly doesn't feel at all accepted where she is, and her mom cannot seem to let it go. She feels like this one issue has formed a wall in the way they relate about anything else. She also feels like her mom doesn't trust the decisions she makes with her own kids. This has brought a wedge in their relationship.

When her mom authoritatively insists, "Those kids need to be in church," Lilly feels like a child. She has so much she would share with her mom about the experiences and dialogue that she and her kids have at home or at the park. Or when they go help someone who is sick and then discuss the "Jesus attitude" they just had by helping and loving someone in need. But her mom can't hear about those precious moments that involve her own grandkids because she's too busy assuming they must all be lost and godless based on church attendance.

We daughters respect your faith, we thank you for the foundation you laid for us, yet we might or might not keep walking on it. But for now, wherever we are, we ask that you respect us enough to not judge where we are spiritually. Or to embrace that there might be other expressions of faith in God than your own denomination or form.

I found God when I went into treatment for alcoholism. I also learned how to let go of my anger and resentment at the church and organized religion by being with other addicts and alcoholics who realized that with resentment, we'll stay miserable. I've learned enough now to know I don't want to judge anyone on the basis of faith—in or out of the church.

You never know what your daughter's spiritual journey will look like or be at any given point, but you've been given your faith—believing what you cannot see—so you won't worry and stress about it. We hope you will trust the process, our process to find our own spirituality without your excessive concern over it.

As daughters, we need to know that you respect the most deeply personal, mysterious thing about us—which is what we think about God. We need to trust that if you profess to be a believer, you will be a *believer* and not a worrier. We want you to know that when you try to control what we believe, it pushes us away and your faith looks weak, even if we know God is strong.

Two-Part Harmony

How can we move toward a mother-daughter duet when we seem so far away from each other in spiritual matters? Christy, a woman in my writers' group, doesn't see eye to eye about a lot of things with her daughter Brittany, including matters of faith. But her mom has learned that even though her daughter's life has ups and downs, she's searching for purpose. Her mom has discovered that the best way to influence her is to let her own life speak, not to obsess about what Brittany's thinking or doing. For years she prayed earnestly for her daughter, yearning for her to change.

But for a time God has seemed much more concerned about working patience and forgiveness in *her own life*.

Christy found that if she preaches, judges, or tries to share Bible verses, it only pushes her daughter away. She becomes a stumbling block, actually hindering Brittany's spiritual journey. She is learning to be more of a stepping stone, building a bridge of understanding by being interested in activities Brittany enjoys.

In the meantime, Christy asks God to bring people into Brittany's life that she'll listen to and gives more attention to learning to reflect Christ's love to her daughter and others. As Christy does, we can start by praying that our lives will reflect his hope, love, and mercy. God is able to make all grace abound to you (2 Corinthians 9:8) so that you can learn to lavish his grace of God on others—especially the beautiful young woman in your life.

We can live our life as an adventure—enjoying daily connection with our Creator and following what he calls us to do, building our own life and enjoying it, going on mission trips or helping people in a social activism program we're passionate about. This kind of purposeful, other-centered living is very appealing to anyone outside the church culture, including a disenchanted daughter.

As we've walked through the last few years of life, Ali and I have reached the point of harmonizing on spiritual matters rather than clashing. We haven't arrived, but we're celebrating what God's doing in the other. Though we each have a very different spiritual language, we can talk about our respective journeys. And in doing so, we have a duet—learning from each other—mother to daughter, adult to adult, pilgrim to pilgrim.

WHEN YOUR DAUGHTER SAYS, "I DO"

The eighth wonder of the world is the
mother-daughter relationship.
—FROM THE MOVIE *BECAUSE I SAID SO*

On December 18, 2000, my sons walked me down the center aisle of the church. Behind the string ensemble, candles glowed as the music started. The bridesmaids in silver dresses walked in one by one. And then as we all stood, our beautiful daughter, Ali, appeared, gliding down the aisle on the arm of her father to the strains of "Jesu, Joy of Man's Desiring."

What happened next no one could have imagined. After the minister's message on the sacred bond of marriage, he started to lead the bride and groom in their wedding vows, but suddenly his words didn't make sense. He couldn't say the bride's and groom's names even though he'd known them for years. After a few minutes that seemed like an eternity, the best man took the pastor's notes and helped the stunned couple finish their vows.

We'd planned that day carefully but just didn't know the minister was going to have a mild stroke right in the middle of Ali and Hans's

ceremony. Though they stayed in their seats, the previously peaceful con-
gregation went into panic mode. After the newlyweds kissed, they headed
for the foyer, and several doctors in the audience sprang to the front of the
church and took the pastor to the hospital.

The time leading up to the wedding wasn't stress free or perfectly
scripted either. One day just before the wedding, I stood in the kitchen
with my to-do list. We were at the countdown phase and had out-of-
town family and friends coming in. I had food to prepare, a house to
clean, clothes to pick up at the cleaners, and a myriad of other things to
do. Before I left for the grocery store and errands, I looked over the items
I needed to do that day.

Ali had just awakened and come in the kitchen to get a cup of coffee. In a sleepy haze, she said, "Mom, why are you so busy?" as she
plopped in a chair. "You're always in task mode. Why don't you chill out
and just relax?"

"Well, honey, we're having a wedding—your wedding—in two
days, and somebody's got to get things done. Then I'll relax after it's over,"
I replied. "Would you like to go with me to do errands?"

"No, I would not. I wish we'd just eloped!" The bride-to-be scowled
as she turned on her heels and traipsed back to her bedroom. I couldn't
imagine why she acted so disinterested. After all, this wedding was for
her and yet she didn't seem to be enjoying the process. The truth was,
neither was I at this point. It was a stretch for me to plan an event—not
my forte—but she and I had made decisions early on based on the budget
we had to work with.

I was baffled and heartsick that day. It surely seemed like my friends
and their daughters got along well during their own wedding planning—and my daughters-in-law and their moms said they enjoyed the
process.

Wedding Stress

An entry in my journal from two weeks before the big day reveals what I was feeling. Our two-year-old granddaughter had just gotten out of the hospital after a bout of pneumonia, I had a pile of work to do, and Christmas was coming—along with the wedding:

> *December 4, 2000*—This seems to be a season of letting go of Ali. I guess God answered my prayer that he would cut all the soul ties and apron strings between us so she could "leave and cleave" to her husband. But I didn't think it'd happen this fast! She seems to be moving away more every day—even though she hasn't moved out yet—spending more time at their apartment, painting rooms, finding just the right lamp to redo. This is so normal, and I love seeing her excitement about their first little home. I'd hoped for some heart-to-heart chats with her before the wedding. But I don't think she's interested. I think she's definitely separating in a big way—normal I know, but still hard. It's a transition. It's like she already slipped away and I hardly got to say good-bye—with no advice for the journey asked for.

When I read Sharon Naylor's online article, "My Mother Is Ruining My Wedding!" I was glad to know we weren't the only mom and daughter who experienced strong emotions or stress. "Weddings stir up underlying issues and intensify family dynamics for anyone, causing the kind of behavior that does injure if not ruin close family ties."[1] Well, even though Ali and I had a nice overnight trip to Tulsa to find her wedding dress and a few other lovely moments together, there were also times when my stressed-out daughter snapped at me or was downright rude. Or I wasn't listening—like in our spat just a few days before the wedding.

I didn't realize that wedding stress affects most mothers and daughters in some way. We just react to it differently. As one mom told me, "My daughter was rude to me on the wedding day. There was so much drama. I was trying not to be hyper hands-on in the planning and went with what she wanted. The wedding was beautiful, but she treated me badly and I couldn't figure out why." Many of the daughters I talked with said their moms were a basket case of nerves, and the mothers said that their daughters cried the night before the wedding and were testy on the big day.

Why are engagements and weddings so emotionally charged? For starters, it's a more final and deep letting go on the mom's part, as I described in my journal entry. So we may feel sadness (I'm losing my daughter, and since she's getting married, I'm getting older) mixed with happiness (her prince has come!) and even a bit of relief (Phew! He'll take care of her and she'll be provided for—especially if he has a good job") or worry (if he doesn't have a good job) and anxiety about the details of the wedding.

If we're honest, it's not just the wedding tension but what it represents. Though we want to be happy our child has found love and commitment, we begin to realize we'll no longer be her next of kin—we're being replaced. As Jane Adams says in *I'm Still Your Mother,* a mother can be very sad when it strikes her that the configuration of people she calls family is about to undergo a drastic revision. "Our position as the most important person in our child's life has been preempted.... The primary bond our grown child has made, legal or putative, replaces the primary one [she] has with us."[2]

There are also a myriad of stress producers for the bride. Her emotions may be all over the map, causing her to be irritable when Mom is only trying to help. She may have the jitters when she thinks about the wedding and cold feet when she ponders the huge lifelong commitment she's about to make. Or Mom may be trying to make it the wedding she never had. Since the most common complaint from brides and their parents is that moms and the brides clash over the wedding planning, what can we do? How do we cope as tension rises?

One way is to be tuned in to our daughters' nonverbal clues and willing to take time from the busyness to listen—which I didn't do well that day. My mind was wrapped up in the details and tasks. When Ali barked at me that morning two days before her wedding because I was "too busy," I didn't see what her real need was—for me to sit down and just ask if she wanted to talk about anything *before* I launched into the to-do list. It may have relieved some tensions.

Apparently I'm not the only one who does this. "Too many mothers get lost in the minutiae of the wedding plans," says Sharon Naylor, wedding specialist and author of more than thirty wedding planning books. "If you focus your gaze on just these to-do items, then you miss the bigger picture of what the whole event is about." Keep the bigger picture in mind. "Think more of the symbolism and meaning of the day than the accoutrements."[3] If you could look inside your daughter's heart, you may find some things that explain her mood swings and outbursts—like being afraid of all the unknowns in her new life.

POTENTIAL FOR DISAPPOINTMENT

There are lots of possibilities for moms to be disappointed with aspects of a daughter's wedding. Sometimes a daughter wants to do everything herself and leaves her mom out. Recently I met a twenty-something woman who decided to pay for her entire wedding and reception and worked an extra job to do so. Her mother had dreams in her head for years about how much fun it would be to plan the wedding *with* her daughter. But her daughter wanted to establish her independence and had different tastes than her mom. Because she did everything herself, mom didn't get to be very involved, and that was a source of hurt and disappointment.

You may have envisioned your daughter marrying the pastor's son in a candlelit church sanctuary with all the family and friends present— while she and her fiancé, who are *not* into doings things the traditional way, decide to marry at the courthouse and spend the money on a fabulous honeymoon. This may create some disappointment and tension. We may not have had our own dream wedding when we were young, so we try to shape our daughters' nuptials into what we always imagined for ourselves—with loving intentions, of course. Added to those emotions, we may be worried about what our relatives and parents will say if the bride doesn't want to wear white and instead concocts her own funky creation to be married in, or if she has her long, silky hair done in dreadlocks.

Perhaps the most difficult disappointment comes when a daughter marries someone we wouldn't have chosen for her. That was true for Gina. In her wildest dreams, she wouldn't have imagined the kind of courtship and wedding her middle daughter would choose. Her oldest daughter married the deacon's son in a traditional wedding at their church. Gina never gave it a thought that Amanda wouldn't follow suit, but nothing could be further from reality.

Instead of meeting her guy at church, Amanda met him on the Internet. One weekend at home, Amanda told her mom all about her new friend. From sharing their journals online in a blog community, she connected with a guy named Shaun, and they'd started e-mailing each other.

"I really, really like Shaun. I think he may be the one, Mom," Amanda told her before leaving.

Gina's anxiety hit the ceiling as she saw her daughter drive away. *My daughter just met him, and she wants to marry him.* She'd heard horror stories of Internet dating and thought this was the most awful thing that could happen. *They haven't even met yet and she's already thinking about a future with this guy?* She hoped and prayed her daughter would lose interest in Shaun.

But the opposite happened. Their Internet relationship blossomed, and the next thing Gina heard he was traveling from his college in Ohio to visit Amanda for a weekend. Then over spring break, they flew to Maryland, where his parents lived, and he proposed. By the time Gina and her husband met Shaun, the couple was already engaged.

Gina hadn't grown up talking to strangers in other states online, and the thought that her daughter was going to marry her Internet boyfriend was scary. So she cautioned her without lambasting the love of her life: "Honey, this is going too fast. Why don't you two wait, slow down? Live in the same state for a while, date and go through the holidays and some real life together. You don't know that much about him! You've only been together a total of three weeks." But her advice was ignored.

Still, she didn't launch a full-court press of opposition against Shaun.

Soon after, they received an e-mail from Shaun asking for their daughter's hand in marriage. He poured out his heart and told how he'd had a serious drug habit and found Christ in rehab; he also expressed his love for their daughter.

They didn't agree with the timing and worried about Amanda marrying a former drug addict, but they knew their strong-willed daughter had made up her mind and they had a choice to make. After much prayer, Gina and her husband decided they'd be there for Amanda regardless, because they loved her unconditionally and never wanted to do anything to break the tie. Gina gave all her expectations to God and let go of her daughter in a deeper way than ever before.

The couple decided on a small wedding—not in their church—but on a cruise ship docked in the Houston port. Since the parents and couple lived in different states it seemed the best way to have both families present, including three sets of grandparents.

The bride was beautiful in a pretty white dress and carried the fresh flower bouquet handed to her by the cruise ship wedding coordinator moments before the wedding. "It was so my free-spirit Amanda who wasn't about the details but the big picture of their relationship," the mother of the bride told me. They had a small reception in the Romeo and Juliet room on ship, and then the newlyweds embarked on a cruise.

Mom could have thrown a fit and refused to give the couple her blessing, but her priority was *connection with her daughter.* Though things didn't go according to her plans, they turned out better than she could have imagined. Several years down the road, she's glad she relied on God instead of on her fears, because what meant the most—relationship with Amanda and Shaun—was not only preserved but grows sweeter by the year.

We're wise when we don't damage the relationship by loudly voicing our opinions and disagreements about the person our child is choosing to marry. When there are genuine concerns (she wants to marry a convicted felon or you've observed the guy's bad temper) we can express them in a loving way—speaking the truth in love—hear our daughter out, and not burn the bridges of relationship.

Also, ask questions (carefully and prayerfully) and listen intently without judging. This can help your daughter think and process what's going on. If you ask good questions at the right time, she is more likely to make wiser decisions. A good rule of thumb for asking questions is to never ask "why" questions. "Why" puts her on the defensive. But a question like, "What do you love the most about him?" could be very revealing to you and to your daughter.

Whatever the situation, we moms need to remember that our daughter's wedding and choice of husband is not about us. It's our daughter's day and marriage, not ours. So if we have been disappointed about our daughter's wedding or choice of a mate, let's release it and be prayerfully supportive and loving as the bride-to-be embarks on a new phase of her life.

A Daughter's Perspective

One of the most anticipated, celebrated days of a girl's life can turn into the biggest nightmare between a bride and her mother. All over a day that will come and go like any other day. First of all, is a wedding more important than a relationship? No. But I think it feels to us daughters like sometimes the wedding takes precedence over us. One bride said, "I've lost all respect for my mother after the way she behaved all through the wedding planning time. She was bossy and selfish. We'll never have a good relationship again."

For mom and me, it's not that anything went particularly wrong in the planning of the wedding; it was more that we were two very different women with different assumptions and ideas during an already stressful, emotionally sensitive time. My mom enjoys people and parties, can start a conversation with just about anyone, anywhere, and doesn't analyze things to death like I do. From the minute Hans and I got engaged, I got nervous about being the center of attention and walking down that long aisle. I toyed with the idea of eloping because it sounded much more up my alley. But with the church culture we were a part of and being the only girl in the family, I thought I owed it to everyone else to have a traditional wedding. Mistake number one on my part: not knowing what I wanted.

So I started listening to anyone and everyone and got more and more anxious. The whole wedding idea proved to be so anxiety-producing that by the time it arrived, most of the simple enjoyment of the event had melted out the church doors before I even got there. I was probably not the most fun daughter to have around through it all. My mom tried to read my mind, please me, and plan together, but I didn't offer much help except snapping at her about this detail and that, taking out my confusion and the pressure I felt on her.

We really had trouble getting on the same page with the whole ordeal. Yes, to me it was an *ordeal*. To her, we were planning a beautiful event. So much of what went into our conflicts over wedding issues was how different our personalities are. Everything became amplified emotionally, I went into antisocial mode being the introvert that I am, and she tried to be my cheerleader and convince me it was fun.

Many days I was excited beyond belief. I was convinced with my heart and soul that I wanted to spend the rest of my life with my best friend and fiancé. All the other details, dates, arrangements, and plans were stressful choices for me to make. Part of me wanted to do it the way my brothers and their wives had—a church wedding with all the trimmings. That's what I thought was expected, and mom went along with that. I was afraid to show the unconventional side of me that wanted to fly away with Hans to Vegas or go downtown to the courthouse and have a party months afterward.

I felt guilty about not being more girly and fun about the planning process. I felt guilty about taking out a lot of my commitment jitters and fears on my mother in the form of snapping or being unappreciative. I felt like I had to be smiley and happy when inside I was a mess.

What I really wanted was my mother's support and listening ear and to disconnect from the preparations, but I didn't know how to say that. My mom wanted things to go well so badly that I didn't feel like I could open up and be honest with some of my not-so-sunshiny feelings. Most of it was nerves, but I really wanted my mom to be able to handle my emotions without getting worried. I wanted to know it was okay and normal to have a myriad of emotions going on along with the joy and bliss.

I wanted to feel safe with the cold-feet feelings or the desire to do something totally unconventional or my fear of being the center of attention. Instead I was afraid because of what I thought a bride was supposed to feel like and act like. I wondered, *Did my mom have any prewedding jitters? Did she and her mom argue about flowers or photographers? Did she feel stressed about costs?* I wanted to hear my mom identify with me or be willing to open up about her experiences, good or bad. I think it might have taken the pressure off a little. And I think I would have felt safe with my queasy reaction to bride season.

Daughters often have conflicting feelings throughout the engagement and wedding planning time. We might act one way and be feeling something completely different but not know how to talk about it. Or if we are frustrated or confused, sometimes we feel pressure to be the perfect bride, without a care in the world. There are so many decisions to make and certain pressures that go along with planning such a memorable day that we feel immensely sensitive to your criticisms or quips. We balk at your opinions because we want to have our own opinions. We want you to encourage us to make our wedding how *we* want it, not how you want it. Coming from you it will mean the world and take the pressure and power struggle off the docket too. We want permission to do it our way, with your input along the way, so that looking back it feels like *our wedding,* not like we got to play a part in your wedding.

My mom and I also both struggled with comparing what we were planning to other weddings we had seen or been a part of. Looking back together on the whole experience, we realized what a deterrent comparison is to fully enjoying the process.

Maybe we daughters are afraid to tell you how we really feel or what we want. We might have doubts or fears about the marriage, and we can't open up to the one person we want to because we're afraid you can't handle it. There are so many decisions, so much potential for stress. And we need you to help us know how to deal with our stress, not pile more on by adding, "You should do it this way." Please don't "should" on us.

My friend Emily shared her experience with her mom, Madge. She and her mother chatted initially about the type of wedding she wanted, the feel and tone of the weekend. But from there, Emily did most of the planning and picking out vendors on the Internet, and a few days before the wedding, the families traveled to Santa Fe. She asked her mom to meet with her and the florist and photographer to tie up loose ends.

Here's what Emily told me: "I don't remember feeling any pressure to make the wedding something that my Mom wanted. It was all about me and Trent, not our moms. But she helped by taking a step back and letting us be ourselves, mistakes and all. We had a little book set out at the reception that guests wrote notes in. Below is the first part of what my Mom wrote:

> AMAZING—When I asked you tonight if your wedding was
> everything you hoped for, you said, "It was amazing!" Now that
> it's over, I must confess that at times it was somewhat difficult for
> me not to have more control in the planning (that's just my nature!). After all, you had never planned an event before—and I
> had. I will never doubt you again. You and Trent did an amazing
> job of planning every little detail of the wedding and party. And
> yes, it was amazing! My hope and prayer for you is that your lives
> together will be equally as amazing as this evening.

Emily felt empowered and encouraged by her mom's belief in her and support of her during such a special time.

As daughters, we want to feel believed in and respected as we begin a whole new chapter of our lives. We want to feel your affirmation of us even if the way we want to plan a wedding is far different from what you did or would do. We want you to be able to enjoy the day, not stress about it, and maybe even say when it's all said and done, "It was amazing." Then let us go when the party's over and take care of yourself. You deserve it.

Lastly, daughters essentially want our moms to be all right either way, whether or not we get married or our approach to the whole question of marriage is entirely different from yours. Whether we're living with our significant others or not dating at all, let us plan and live our own lives.

WHOSE DREAM WEDDING IS IT?

Here is another way to approach wedding planning: one that hurts the relationship and the other that builds the mom-daughter connection.

Stephanie and her mother had been close through high school and college. Even in college, they talked every day and saw each other often. But when she got engaged, a drastic change occurred. Listen in as Stephanie explains:

> My mom was devoted to me and my siblings. But when I got
> engaged and she was devastated, I realized she'd put me in an
> unhealthy place—the center of her world—and didn't want to
> let me go. She took it personally that I was getting married, like
> I was deserting her. I felt I had a lot of responsibility to bear that
> wasn't mine, and it made me feel guilty.
>
> Mom became very controlling and combative. She wanted
> to control me and every aspect of the wedding plans. So the en-
> gagement was framed by our fights. In my whole lifetime, it was
> the worst time of our relationship. I was marrying a wonderful
> man and wanted us to enjoy this time, but she argued about

every detail: the colors of the wedding, the kind of flowers and cake. Whatever I chose, she turned her nose up at, so finally I began to comply with what pleased her. She wanted to give me a dream wedding, but it was her dream wedding, not mine.

We fought at all my showers; she didn't like my attitude. Or some petty thing happened and it escalated into World War III. Finally I was so miserable one day, I knew I had to release my wedding to God to have any peace at all. It was hard, but I laid it down.

Because I released it and let her do it her way, I enjoyed the wedding. Mom was completely stressed out that day. I appreciated all her efforts, but it wasn't my dream wedding—it really was hers. And I was so glad when it was over.

Hearing this young woman, I was struck by the fact that it wasn't really the bride's job to let go of the wedding. It was her mom's place to let go and let God. Underneath all her control were many longings and unmet expectations mixed with anger at her daughter for leaving her. What a recipe for conflict!

And instead of the wedding drawing them closer, it created distance that is still in the process of being worked out today. Mom got her way, but she was too stressed to really enjoy the day—which is what happens when we're trying to control things. Finally, two years after the wedding, when her mom came to see her first child, Stephanie told her what she'd felt. Her mom said she was sorry she'd controlled everything and explained she was feeling so abandoned that she clung to Stephanie as her security, that she was in a lot of pain and fear, so she tried to control.

Just a tip: if you apologize, as Stephanie's mother did, try not to make excuses and rationalize your actions. ("I was just lonely; I felt I was losing you so I controlled the wedding, did things my way, and fought with you…") I know from experience it's so easy for us as moms to justify and defend ourselves, which leads our daughters to more resentment instead of bringing peace between us. It's best to just say, "I was wrong, and I have no excuses. Please forgive me."

Two-Part Harmony

When Ali and I relived the engagement and wedding time and compared stories and perspectives ten years later, we reveled in the redemptive aspect of life. I recalled how after Ali and Hans had left for their honeymoon and we were packing up the centerpieces and reception decorations, I got a phone call from her.

"Mom, I just wanted to say thank you for all you did for the wedding to happen. I didn't realize everything that had to be done for it to come together, but it was beautiful. You were so wonderful to do all that—and the coffee bar was awesome. I've been so ungrateful and I'm sorry. I just wanted you to know how much I appreciate what you did."

As we looked at the wedding pictures, sweet memories swept into our minds. The moment when the flower girls, Caitlin and Jesika, two and four years old, strolled down the aisle tossing rose petals. How Hans's smile lit up the room when he saw Ali. The family members on both sides who drove from Texas and Arkansas in winter weather to be there. The classical guitarist and espresso bar Ali had envisioned. Even with the tension we'd had and unavoidable things that happened, processing the whole thing together by focusing on gratefulness transformed the experience for both of us.

Time heals wounds, but it also helps us make sense of things. We look back now with empathy for what the other was going through. We admit where we were and how we related out of our pain and lack of understanding. We can see the behind-the-scenes aspects of that chaotic time and realize how much we've grown. We can extend forgiveness and mercy to each other now. And from it we've learned to put ourselves into each other's shoes during chaotic times or big transitions. When you're looking toward your daughter's future wedding, remember how important it is to savor the moments and enjoy them. That may be difficult if you have a tendency to get in task mode, focusing on all the things you still have to check off your to-do list. If so, you might find it helpful to pray daily, *"Lord, help me to let go and enjoy this day, each moment of today during this changing season. Show me what really matters and help me give grace to my daughter."*

This is an opportunity to build your mother-daughter bond and be a source of peace, not added pressure to your daughter. Be a safe place for your daughter to communicate the myriad of feelings and emotions that will come up during the engagement and wedding planning. Then no matter how she plans this wedding day or how it turns out, you will both be brought closer in the process. If you keep things in perspective, you can help create a no-fail mood that will empower and encourage your daughter in this new chapter of her life.

NOW THAT SHE'S A MOM

· · · · ·

She was born to me and she was born a girl. And I
was born to my mother and I was born a girl. All of
us are like stairs, one step after another, going up
and down, but all going the same way.

—AMY TAN, *THE JOY LUCK CLUB*

· · · · ·

We were pacing around in the hall of the maternity floor, holding a bright bunch of "Congratulations" balloons, wondering what Ali's baby was going to look like. Would he have blue eyes or brown? blond hair or dark hair? As it turned out, Noah had a beautiful head of red hair. Seeing his bright blue eyes, alert even in the first moments on earth, sent a wave of joy through me.

When they came home from the hospital, I helped Ali for a few days until I felt I was underfoot and the new mom, dad, and baby boy were settled in. In the next few weeks I popped by to pick up laundry, bring a meal, or bring something Ali needed from the pharmacy. When I was with them, I loved holding my precious grandboy, Noah.

Like many other moms from my generation, I said the taboo words and phrases destined to offend the new mom. I wish I'd said all the right, supportive things to Ali, but I did not.

When she was nervous about breastfeeding, I tried to be encouraging and told her, "Breastfeeding is just so natural; all my sisters and I nursed our babies, and it'll be just fine for you too. When you were a baby, I loved rocking you in the yellow rocker and nursing you. Those were peaceful moments."

However, breastfeeding was just the opposite for her. Ali did nurse for nine months, but some physiological obstacles made nursing difficult and painful. I didn't know she'd compare herself to my experiences and feel inadequate. I learned by trial and error that speaking thoughtlessly, comparing the new mom to ourselves or anyone else is a surefire way to make her hopping mad or hurt her feelings.

When Ali was up all night with a baby who wouldn't sleep, I put my foot in my mouth again and said, "All three of you slept all night when you were about a month old." Jab—right in her heart. It was not helpful to Ali. Though I don't like admitting my thoughtless remarks, maybe it will save some mother reading this book from making the same mistake.

When our daughter becomes a mother, it's quite a transition for both of us. She has all the emotions and responsibilities and thoughts that 24/7 care of a child entails. And wonder of wonders—we have become grandparents! Whether you decide to call yourself "Mimi" or "Nana" or just wait for the baby to decide your name when he or she starts talking, you take on a new role. Most grandmas I know are a little delirious with joy when the first grandchild arrives. We may carry a giant stack of photos in our purse, just waiting to hop on some unsuspecting person who asks about our family's new arrival. Then we whip out pictures of our cute grandson or granddaughter. We e-mail our out-of-town friends to announce the birth and offer to baby-sit almost anytime.

In the midst of the joy we experience with grandchildren are all kinds of possibilities for new tensions between mother and daughter, not just in the expecting phase and new baby stage, but throughout her parenting experience.

Sometimes the birth of a child can bring mother and daughter into a better relationship. Other times, new tensions erupt, as was the case with one woman I interviewed who said, "I don't get to really enjoy the grandkids as I'd wanted. I'd like to be closer to them, but my daughter has lots and lots of parameters and rules: you can do this, you can't do that with them. I need to be allowed to be who I am and not feel criticized and scrutinized. It's very hurtful to have this going on; it's formed a barrier in our relationship."

WHAT NOT TO SAY

You may be wondering, *What are the wrong things to say? When do I give advice? How can I be most helpful and supportive to my daughter?* James 1:19 was meant especially for us moms: "Be quick to listen, slow to speak and slow to become angry."

Here's what Cynthia, a mother of four told me. "When I first became a parent, mom's initial parenting advice really hurt my feelings. I wasn't getting any sleep and the baby was colicky. When I was telling her about it, she said, 'Oh, here's what you do to get him to stay asleep...,' which only made me feel inept and didn't solve anything. All I wanted her to say was something like, 'I know it's hard,' to affirm where I was and commiserate a little."

Cynthia finally got enough courage to say, "That's not helpful, Mom." Cynthia was grateful that her mother was open to her feedback about what responses weren't helpful and not oversensitive about her own mistakes. (A good role model for all of us, don't you think?)

We moms need the wisdom to speak words at the right time, "gentle words [which] are a tree of life" (Proverbs 15:4, NLT), rather than saying things like, "Why aren't you taking your child to church every Sunday?" or "His hair looks dry. What are you washing it with?" It takes a lot of restraint and grace, trusting God that he's the one with the answers, not us, and that our daughters will figure things out—whether it's how to deal with a colicky baby who won't take naps, a toddler who avoids potty training, or an elementary school child who is struggling in math.

A friend of mine's mother majored in being critical and carried that right into her daughter's parenting years. For instance, this grandmother arrived for a visit at her daughter's house and hadn't seen little Jason for three years. Grandma looked at the six-year-old and said, "He's so fat!" instead of, "Hi, honey—so good to see you!" Needless to say, he—and his mom—were hurt. This mother expected her daughter to serve her and take care of her needs when she came to visit, yet her overloaded daughter was already caring for a household and three young children. No wonder the family didn't look forward to Grandma's visits.

As moms, we can go to our daughters' homes with an attitude of "How can I serve and bless you and your family?" especially if we are going to stay for a week or more. We can purpose to be warm and positive, not critical and negative about the kids or how our daughter and her husband are raising them. I've learned the greatest thing we can do to respect their parenting is to do what they ask: if it's dietary matters, follow the diet, and if they don't allow the kids to watch certain TV shows, support that and don't let them watch the programs when they're in your care. Then we will be a blessing and support to our daughters—and they will feel our love and respect.

Sometimes our words aren't a problem, but our timing is. That's what happened when Ruthie's mom called one day when her boys were young. Her first son was twenty-eight months old and his darling new brother was what she called a "barfing baby." If Daniel was happy, he threw up. If he had a fever, he threw up. If he was cutting a tooth…you guessed it.

She was already having a bad day because Daniel wasn't only barfing but having diarrhea to boot.

Ruthie was racing around the kitchen when suddenly the phone rang. As she balanced her baby on her hip, she heard her mom ask, "How are you? What's going on?"

"Well, I'm trying to get dinner ready before Tim comes home, and Daniel has thrown up four times, and I've had to change my clothes three times." Ruthie answered with a slight edge to her voice.

"Oh honey, just *enjoy it,*" Mom responded. Ruthie was so frustrated and mad, she almost hung up on her mom. Her mother was probably just trying to cheer her daughter up, but maybe she wasn't listening to the crying baby, the clanging pots and pans, or the distressed tone of her daughter's voice. If she had, she might have realized her daughter needed her empathy and her ear. Instead, she said something that minimized her daughter's understandable frustration.

WHEN TO GIVE ADVICE AND ASSURANCE

We affirm new mothers when we back off a bit and allow them to figure things out for themselves, when we are concerned but not intrusive, which demonstrates that we trust them to care for the baby. One mom said, "I appreciated my mom's hands-off attitude when I had my first baby. We were living with them, but when I was deciding whether to stop breast-feeding or when my baby screamed with colic, she didn't interfere. She let me ask for help when I wanted it."

Courtney, a wise mother and grandma I know, told me that she decided when her first grandson was born she'd be available when her daughter asked for advice and that she would not dive in and try to fix things or give unsolicited suggestions. If her daughter was gushing about the baby wanting to eat every hour and a half or that her seven-year-old was difficult to discipline, Courtney listened and heard her out first. She didn't jump in and say, "You ought to do this," or "This worked for me." Instead she took a step back to consider whether her daughter just needed someone to listen or really wanted some help looking at options. If she wasn't sure if her daughter was asking her opinion, she might ask:

- Would you like to know what I might do? (This way, she asked permission to share some wisdom instead of dumping unwanted information on her.)
- Would you like to look at what you're doing and what's working and not working?
- Is there anything I can do to help you process this?

If her daughter said things like, "Mom, I've tried this method of discipline and read this book and nothing's helped. I'm just tired of it all and am doing a terrible job as a mom!" Courtney didn't claim to have all the answers or get out her favorite parenting book and read advice to her daughter.

Courtney responded to her daughter as a mother and an adult in her own right. She respected her daughter's parenting, even when it was different than her own, instead of criticizing. As a result the message she sent to her daughter was this: *I don't want to fix this for you. I know you'll figure it out.*

Sometimes our daughters just need assurance from us. For instance, let's say your daughter calls, saying that the kids have been fighting with each other all week. They've all been sick and cranky and are driving her crazy. You stop by her house to bring some chicken noodle soup and Gatorade when she has a meltdown and cries about her frustrations. "I don't think I'm a good enough mom! I've been impatient and yelled at the kids twice today. I don't want them to be messed up by my not doing a good job of parenting."

At that point, your daughter doesn't need for you to heap guilt upon the guilt she already feels or to toss out easy answers. Maybe she just needs you to offer assurance, like "Oh honey, you're a good mom or you wouldn't be worrying about this. You have a wonderful heart for your children and are investing so much love in their lives."

You can validate her feelings by saying, "I remember feeling like that too. This is normal. You're tired because you were up all night with the toddler, you're working part time to make ends meet, and you're discouraged. But you're doing a wonderful job."

If you were that daughter, can't you just imagine the relief you'd feel, how thankful you'd be for those kind words of assurance when you needed them the most? Letting our daughters know that there's no perfect way to raise kids, no manual for fool-proof, nonstressful mothering practices, and assuring them that no one can tell you exactly how it's going to be or what to do is of great value.

I've learned through trial and error *not* to give advice unless it's asked for and to "keep my mouth shut and my feet on God's path." I've learned and *know* that my adult children and their spouses will figure it out (whatever "it" is), and do very well without any intervention from me. In fact, I stand back and marvel at how well they're handling life, what good planners they are, how much they love each other and their kids, and how they take care of them with such devotion and commitment. I really admire the adults they've become.

WHAT IF YOUR DAUGHTER THINKS YOU AREN'T DOING ENOUGH?

Grandmas love their grandchildren; we don't even have to work at it. But sometimes your daughter expects more involvement than you're capable of. Maybe her friends' moms are supergrandmas. Or she has high expectations of what a grandma is supposed to be, as Ann did. She expected her mom to baby-sit often and let her kids camp out at her house two week-ends a month—even though her mom worked full time, was tired on the weekends, and had all her own household duties waiting. When Ann asked her mom to baby-sit on the weekends and she didn't say yes, Ann got angry.

She was also hurt and disappointed and tried to guilt her mom into more time with her kids. Her mom just didn't match up to Ann's vision of a doting grandma. But when emotions simmered down, she and her mother talked, and Ann told her mom that what she really wanted was for her kids to know their grandmother. When her mom realized this, it motivated her to do what she could without sacrificing much-needed weekend sleep. Ann's mom set some healthy boundaries about how much she could have the grandkids over. In turn, Ann's respect for her mom grew and their relationship was strengthened.

Hearing your daughter's real need ("I want my kids to know you") and speaking your heart ("I love my grandchildren and want to spend time with them, but I have to pace myself because I have a life too") are important keys to navigating this complexity in a mother-daughter relationship.

WHEN YOU'RE CONCERNED

Sometimes we mothers and grandmas see things our daughters are doing with their kids that concern us. We pray about it and give it to God and walk away, trusting they will handle it. But other times we need to speak up. It's a risk, but there are times a mom will speak to her daughter be-cause of her love for her grandchild.

"We have rules at our house, and they have rules at their house," said Gretchen. "And I try to respect the decisions my daughter and her hus-band make as they're raising their two- and four-year-olds and affirm them whenever I can. I seldom step in and say anything. But on the few times I have, they tend to listen because it's so rare."

One of those times was when her daughter Paula and her husband, Don, arrived to drop off their kids. Tensions were high because Don's grandfather had died and the family had been to the funeral. As the family was talking, four-year-old Jimmy wanted something and was jumping around. Paula yelled, "Don't you realize that your grandfather is dead and we're all dealing with it!" In the next few moments Gretchen considered whether to say anything. Other times when she disagreed with how Paula and Don handled something, she had sensed she just needed to keep quiet and pray about it. But not this time. Gretchen asked Paula if she could talk to her in the kitchen.

"Paula, he's just four years old. He doesn't understand everything you two are going through. He's just being a kid."

"Maybe you're right, Mom. I know we're hard on him, maybe because he's so smart we treat him like he's older." After some cooling-off moments, Paula returned to the living room and apologized to Jimmy. (A caution here: if you disagree about something your daughter is doing, talk to her directly and apart from her children, as this mom and grandma did.)

POSTPARTUM DEPRESSION

Some women struggle with depression after giving birth. In fact, postpartum depression is more common than I realized. Perhaps that's why I didn't pick up the clues when Ali was looking so sad after the birth of her second little boy. I didn't know the symptoms; at that time, there was not much written about postpartum depression (PPD). Even the obstetricians in our city had little understanding of the condition or what to do to help these mothers. I'd heard of "the baby blues" and had experienced some of those feelings myself after my first two births, but I figured that Ali's low mood might be because she was severely sleep-deprived and hormonal. Luke didn't particularly like being a baby or sleeping at night.

Her sadness wasn't just for a few days or weeks; it persisted for months. I was very concerned. When I tried to talk with her, she shut down and said I didn't understand, that my babies had done just fine and slept all night. When I suggested she talk to her doctor about how she was feeling, she felt criticized and cried. It was a challenging time for all of us. Since Ali and Hans were living with us, I was swamped during the day with laundry, making breakfast, lunch, and dinner for the family, and helping care for Noah while his daddy was at work. Plus, whenever I could, I went to my office to work. But there were also moments of grace, moments spent with Noah while his parents were at the hospital with his baby brother, taking Noah to McDonald's for a Happy Meal and toy and then to the park to play since he missed Mommy so much.

No wonder I missed Ali's symptoms of postpartum depression. Her doctor missed them as well. I've since learned that symptoms include being restless or irritable, withdrawing from activities, sleeping disturbances, feeling sad or helpless, trouble focusing, memory problems, no energy or motivation, and crying a lot. These are all part of the mood disorder. I just wish I'd had more knowledge and that Ali had gotten help sooner. Though her onset of postpartum depression was during the first few months, mothers are at risk for this condition for up to a year after giving birth.

If you observe this cluster of symptoms in your daughter, do some reading and research before saying anything. Be sensitive, proceed gently and cautiously, but please get her some help if the PPD doesn't resolve itself. Treatments such as talk therapy and medication can be effective in treating the condition so the mom returns to mental and emotional health.

As Ali explains in her part of the story, a number of months later we went to a seminar at the National Mother of the Year convention in Puerto Rico, not knowing that the subject was on postpartum depression and the speaker's experience. During that hour, the speaker explained how she'd suffered with a case of postpartum depression so serious her family had her committed to a psychiatric hospital, how she'd searched all over her state and finally found an obstetrician in California who specialized in treatment for this condition. Coincidentally, this woman lived right in Oklahoma City, and she and Ali went to the same doctor. Ali and I had a chance to talk with her, and she graciously took Ali under her wing, giving her information on how to talk to her doctor and ask for treatment. I'll let her tell you the rest of the story.

A Daughter's Perspective

I struggled with baby blues a bit after my first baby, but the clincher came when Noah was nine months old, and I found out I was pregnant again. Dismay and disbelief filled me when I saw the little blue line. I was on the pill and still nursing and had assumed I couldn't get pregnant. I fell apart at mom's house and lay in the fetal position overwhelmed with feelings. Hans was looking for a job, and we were staying with my parents until we could get on our feet. It was a scary time, and I felt so inadequate. I didn't know how to put words to the feelings, and I kept comparing myself to my mom, who had always appeared to have shone like a star in the area of childbearing and child rearing. She seemed to excel in most domestic ways, cooking, and keeping things organized. I was completely domestically challenged. Two babies back to back? I felt I didn't have whatever it took to be "good enough" to do the job.

My mom and I experienced motherhood in completely different ways. She gave birth without meds; I asked for the epidural before I was checked in. She liked breastfeeding, and it came naturally to her and all her sisters; I, on the other hand, was "lactationally challenged." Breastfeeding might have been the hardest thing I have ever done.

I got frustrated and hypersensitive when Mom would volunteer her experience or offer a word of advice. I know now that she was trying to help, but I was quite reactive to simple innocent comments. I felt at times like I had a chip missing designed for the enjoyment of pregnancy, childbirth, nursing, especially in the first few months. The baby season was not my cup of tea. In addition, I struggled with copious weight gain. Mom had not.

Deep down I wanted her to open up and tell me she understood. I wanted her to open up and candidly share the struggles of her motherhood experience and her foibles as a mom so that I didn't feel so alone in mine. But maybe her experience really was different; maybe she could not understand. If so, how was she going to be able to go there with me?

I found myself enveloped in a sea of inexpressible sadness, anxiety, confusion. Everything went dark and I couldn't seem to shake off whatever had enveloped me. Luckily, once I finally got help, things started turning around slowly but surely. Tensions eased between my mom and me after I got the help and medication I needed to get me back to a functioning place. Mom finally understood that she alone couldn't fix me or get me out of the funk. When I really needed her, she was totally there. Once we realized I was suffering from postpartum depression, she was my champion for getting help. She became more and more present and offered advice less and less.

Becoming a mother can be a crazy hard transition, even when a daughter's experience as a mom isn't complicated by postpartum depression, as mine was. And although your daughter's circumstances may be different, she still wants to be respected. Maybe we are single parents, maybe we are married, maybe we planned the baby, and maybe we didn't.

No matter our situation, we have made the shift and we are now mothers, not just daughters.

While we respect you for having done motherhood, for all your sacrifices, and are grateful, we want you to realize that it's our turn now. It's our turn to be exhausted after sleepless nights. We don't need advice—unless we ask you for it—but we might need a meal. We don't need a list of how-tos and "here's what I did" (unless we ask for it), but we might need an encouraging word about how you see that we are doing a good job even though we're exhausted. We want you to realize that as sacred as your experience of parenting us was to you, our experience with our kids is sacred to us. We need for you to respect that and to know that you understand we are not babies anymore and that our experience as moms is going to be different from yours. Even our perspective on parenting may be different.

The words you say make a difference. I've heard many daughters say, "I wish my mom could just be real and tell me she felt exhausted like I did" or "All I hear from my mom is what I'm not doing right." When you say things like, "Now listen, I know how to do it. After all, I raised you and your sisters," or "If you do it this way, it will help you get more sleep" (or your kid will be calmer or smarter or better adjusted), it makes us feel inferior and frustrated.

It feels as if the rug is pulled out from under us before we even figure out how to make our own mother mark. We're creating our own tune, our own lullaby between ourselves and our children. When you try to sing your tune, it clashes; it's a different song altogether. Then it feels the opposite of a lullaby; it feels like a clashing cymbal while we're trying to put our family to bed.

When we hear your voice and advice constantly, it causes us to doubt ourselves. We don't take confidence in our own nurturing abilities if you are constantly compelled to critique. At times your input is like water in a desert, but if it's not wrapped in love or genuine encouragement or if you take it personally when we don't respond with, "Oh thank you! You are the überknowledgeable one!" then it will create distance, and we won't feel safe sharing our sacred experience with you.

We love it when you delight in our newfound strengths when we become mothers ourselves. We love it when you tell us you are proud of us and leave it at that. We love it when you offer practical help without advice. We love when you help the first two weeks after we give birth with an extra lot of grace and support. We love it when you don't guilt us with how much you see or don't see our children. We love it when you want to interact with us, even if it has nothing to do with talking about the kids and parenting issues. We love watching you become grandmothers and seeing our kids adore you and know you. We love you. We are grateful for your example. Now let us set the example for our children. Please let us be mothers ourselves.

Two-Part Harmony

Since our experiences with parenting may be different from our daughters', it helps to consider: how would you treat a friend who just had a baby? Perhaps you'd bring a meal and talk softly and compliment her and ask, "Is there anything you need?" Then you would probably hop back in your car, drive home, and trust your friend will be okay when you leave and that she'll be able to take care of her child just fine. Our daughters are deflated in response to our worry and empowered by our peace of mind.

If as a single woman your daughter chooses to adopt a child, she needs you to trust her process of arriving at those decisions. Or if she plans on a home birth in a bathtub with a midwife assisting, support her in that decision. It's the same when she decides to go back to work, or what time and how she puts her kids to bed, or what kind of discipline she decides to utilize with her children. She is thinking through all these decisions, just as you once did. But her personality is different from yours, her world is different, her generation is different, and different is *good*, not bad.

(Ali speaking:) While my mom said the wrong things on several occasions during the baby phase, she accepted and encouraged my every move when it came to my parenting methods. When my husband and I were feeling pressure from our surroundings to implement some specific parenting methods, I felt conflicted and pressured to follow suit. I felt that I could express that stress to my mom and describe how I loved doing what we were doing, how it was working for us. I didn't hear one word of criticism from her or one splash of advice.

At that point she taught me how to be a mother by showing her acceptance and ability to listen without judgment, to affirm, "Yes, I believe in you. I believe in your ability to figure out what works for you, and I'm proud of you for doing it the way that works for you." I felt so inadequate with each stage in those first few years, and what buoyed me out of that place was her insistence that I knew my boys better than anyone. By her consistent actions and verbal affirmations I found out she believed in me to be able to do this parent thing, even though I was her baby. And once I realized that, I began to believe in myself.

(Cheri speaking:) Even if daughters whine about sleepless nights or make mistakes while finding their own methods of parenting, they still need to feel that we're letting go of our expectations and trusting God with them. While our daughters are working out the kinks, let's be patient and bring them a coffee with no advice or strings attached. That one always worked wonders for Ali.

We think you'll find your daughter will invite you into the picture with much more willingness and ease if you come in advice free, willing to be real with your own foibles as a mom, a little humor, and maybe a tasty treat. You may also find that as a result of being a mother, she may see you in a new light, become more appreciative of all you did to raise her, and your relationship will grow in new ways.

WHEN CRISIS ARISES

· · · · ·

Crises refine life. In them you discover what you are.
—ALLAN K. CHALMERS

· · · · ·

Remember when our daughters were toddlers and a Band-Aid, a kiss, and hug would ease the pain of their hurts and boo-boos? I remember one day when Ali fell off her blue bike with training wheels as she tried to keep up with her brothers on their dirt bikes. Hearing her scream, I ran out to the sidewalk, scooped her up, and took her into the house. I sat her up on the bathroom counter and blew on the abrasion (though there was nothing medicinal about it, just something we moms do). Then I gently washed the scrape and though she protested, put on some antibiotic cream.

"There, honey, it will be better in a little while," I said as we went into the kitchen and I poured her some apple juice.

But what about when this little daughter is an adult and she is struggling with bulimia, or her marriage is ending, or she's lost her job and apartment, or she's in a crisis pregnancy or struggling with an addiction? If only we could ease the pain of those experiences as easily as we did when she was a little girl. As moms we want desperately to do something. But no Band-Aid can patch the huge, gaping wound in her heart.

I stopped by my daughter's house one gray, rainy day to drop off a cup of Starbucks and some Pampers. The boys were napping, and I moved some clean laundry off the brown couch to sit near Ali. Her sad expression spoke volumes, and I ached for the unhappiness and turmoil she was going through. I wanted to comfort her because I knew the pain of a detached, strained marriage and how alone I'd felt.

I could tell from the dark circles that she wasn't getting enough sleep. The weeks before, thoughts had gone through my mind like a tape recorder playing, *I wish I could help. I wish I could do something.* By this time I'd found that writing how-to books on parenting and education had its downside: that of being a solution-oriented, brimming-over-with-ideas-for-fixing-things mother.

In the past when she'd had bouts of depression, I'd tried things like giving her an article from a magazine, sharing my Ziploc bag full of Bible verses, or trying to give her a pep talk, and it didn't do anything except cause her to distance herself from me. I also knew giving my opinion wasn't going to help. Neither would talking or comparing her situation to troubles her father and I had gone through in our marriage—or any-one else's.

After we talked, I drove home and slipped to my knees in the bed-room, my heart heavy. I'd said so many prayers I was about prayed out. *What's your plan, God? Am I not praying in the right way? My prayers seem to be bouncing off the ceiling and falling to the ground without any effect. How are you praying for them?* I asked, believing that Jesus really was in heaven, praying for them too, and maybe he'd give me some assistance here (see Hebrews 7:25). I sure needed it. I didn't want to help God out or suggest an agenda to him, but I was so frustrated and discouraged with Ali's struggles with depression and her strained marriage. I waited and waited for a glimpse of light, a verse, or a bit of insight.

But insight wasn't what I got—at least not the kind I expected.

Suddenly I felt an overwhelming sense of helplessness. Just pure, utter, and complete helplessness. Tears slipped down my cheeks as I wept for my daughter and for my own inability and lack of wisdom. No words came; no prayers were said.

Slowly as I knelt there with all that helplessness sinking in to a deeper place than I'd ever felt, something came to mind that I'd read in O. Hallesby's book *Prayer,* about how helplessness is our best prayer and even a gift.

What a strange thought. *Helplessness—a gift?* I knew I didn't conjure up that thought. As moms we want to *do something* to stop the hurting if our child is in pain. But I couldn't, and it felt *awful.* It felt humbling to be so weak and inadequate. Everything in me wanted to do something to help, even pray the right way, but I felt that I was failing. I had to find what else Hallesby said about helplessness, so I got the well-worn paperback off my nightstand.

> Helplessness is the real secret and the impelling power of prayer.
> You should therefore rather try to thank God for the feeling of
> helplessness which He has given you. It is one of the greatest
> gifts which God can impart to us. For it is only when we are
> helpless that we open our hearts to Jesus and let Him help us
> in our distress.[1]

Thank God for helplessness? Not exactly what I'd been thinking. The next few paragraphs gripped me:

> If you are a mother, you will understand this, too, better than the
> rest of us. You care for your little ones night and day, even though
> they do not understand what you are doing, sacrificing and suf-
> fering for them. They do not thank you, and often they are even

contrary, causing you not a little difficulty. But you do not let
that hinder you. You hear and answer incessantly the prayer
which their helplessness sends up to your mother-heart.

Such is God.

Only that He does perfectly what human love can only do
imperfectly. As a true mother dedicates her life to the care of her
children, so the eternal God in His infinite mercy has dedicated
Himself eternally to the care of His frail and erring children.[2]

Those words brought a strange comfort to me. The Lord was going
to take care of my daughter and her family. I didn't need to do anything
but trust him and let go, bringing them to him in prayer—but *not go pick
them up later* and try to "help God." As I pondered that thought, my
heart finally rested and I felt peace. I got up knowing that God could
handle not only Ali's present troubles but also anything she might face in
the future. I didn't know what the process was going to be, but I had to
step back and let the process work itself out. My part was to keep letting
go of what I couldn't control, day by day and sometimes moment by moment, to keep loving these precious ones, no matter what happened.

Some days the letting go was easier, and other days I struggled to do
so. One of those mornings, when I was back into doing something to
help, I thought, *Maybe I'll just drive to Hans's office and go talk some sense
into my son-in-law. I want them to work this out! To tell Hans what a jewel
his wife is and how lucky he is and that if they just worked on their marriage
everything would work out*—or something positive like that. My husband
didn't think it was a good idea, but I proceeded with those thoughts over
breakfast. When I had some quiet time, even though I hadn't asked him,
I distinctly heard God say, "Don't you do that." Next I heard, "Go to
Hans's office, but don't say a word of advice. Just go in and give him a hug
and tell him you love him." Not what I'd planned.

When I drove up and walked in my son-in-law's office, it took everything in me to not say any words of advice, even well-meant. After extending a hug, I told him I loved him, walked out, and drove home.

It took months for their marriage to be repaired; it was not a straight shot to marital bliss. Yet God was more creative than I could have imagined, and slowly, through means Hans and Ali chose and ways beyond my understanding, their hearts began to be knit back together. As I watched, prayed, and cheered from the sidelines, this I learned: God didn't need me to direct the process. He just needed me to love them, trust him, and be very patient. Instead of feeling resentful that I'd taken sides, criticized her husband or her way of handling things, or given her advice that made things worse, Ali sensed my support and love, and that's what she really needed.

WHEN THE "WORST" HAPPENS

Liz's daughter started rebelling when she was a teenager, and her rebellion was in full-court-press craziness by the time she turned twenty-one years old. She had tattoos up and down her arms and lived with a raunchy group of people in an apartment two hours away from her parents. They'd raised her in a loving Christian home and given her every advantage and tried everything to help her—taking her to a family counselor, asking their pastor for advice, praying with other parents of prodigals—but nothing worked.

The day Liz got the news from her daughter that she was pregnant, she thought she'd tear her hair out. Surely this was the worst thing that could happen. "Mom, I've done five different pregnancy tests, and they all came out positive."

Liz's heart sunk and anger erupted, "You're unmarried, you have no money, you've been taking drugs and live with unemployed losers about one step from homelessness. How sad to bring a child into this kind of a life…" When her daughter tried to say something, Liz reamed into her, "You're not going to marry that guy, are you? You ought to give it up for adoption—" Just then her daughter hung up. Liz promptly regretted her tirade, not because it wasn't true but because it only further pushed her troubled daughter away.

Eight months passed and mother and daughter saw each other a few times during the pregnancy. Liz hadn't experienced a big turnaround in her attitude about the pregnancy, and she didn't feel hopeful about her daughter's or the baby's situation.

In the end, or shall we say the beginning, against Mom and Dad's advice, her daughter decided to keep the baby. When she saw the ultrasound at nineteen weeks, something began to change. She'd already quit alcohol and drugs but now started consciously taking better care of herself. She got some prenatal vitamins and a part-time job and moved in with a girlfriend she'd known in high school who was better company.

What Liz thought was the "worst thing" turned out to be the best thing for her daughter. She gave birth to a healthy baby girl and slowly began seeing her mother in a different light now that she was a parent. For the first time, she appreciated her mom and even called to ask her questions when the baby was sick or she was having a hard day. Her daughter's and granddaughter's futures weren't secure and there were still lots of concerns, but what no counselor, pastor, or parent could do to help her daughter desire a healthier lifestyle, a little eight-pound girl did.

When I talked with Liz a year after her daughter's baby was born, she told me how much she'd learned and how she regretted reacting before she'd even heard her daughter out in their first conversation. She'd judged and felt right and was shocked and gripped by fear for the child and her daughter, and she felt sadness any mom would feel, but lashing out at her daughter had only made them both feel miserable.

I was struck recently by what Melody Beattie, author of *Codependent No More,* said about reacting.

> Reacting usually does not work. We react too quickly, with too much intensity and urgency. Rarely can we do our best at anything in this state of mind. I believe the irony is that we are not called upon or required to do things in this state of mind. There is little in our lives we need to do that we cannot do better if we are peaceful. Few situations—no matter how greatly they appear to demand it—can be bettered by us going berserk.
>
> Why do we do it, then?
>
> We react because we're anxious and afraid of what has happened, what might happen, and what is happening....
>
> We react because we think things *shouldn't* be happening the way they are.
>
> We react because we don't feel good about ourselves.[3]

Maybe Liz had reacted because she felt she'd somehow failed as a mother. It had been hard enough to face the stares and hear the questions when other women at church found out about her daughter's drug use or asked where she was. (Her parents hadn't always known.) Now Liz knew they'd be gossiping about the unwed mother. But the more she worried about what others would say, the more she realized caring so much about what they thought was *her own problem* to work on.

Liz also learned what helped and what didn't. What didn't help was telling her daughter what to do and trying to control her life. Nor did it develop a stronger connection between them. What did help was to practice some detachment from her daughter and her embroilments. This kind of detachment doesn't mean you're not loving the person; you can still love your daughter without liking her behavior. It means letting go of our obsession with her (or another's) behavior and not letting ourselves be used and abused by her. It means not covering up her mistakes or manipulating situations so that she won't experience consequences. It means getting get out of the way and leading our own lives.

It was a struggle at first to detach, but Liz found she needed to pay attention to her own life instead of being so obsessed with her daughter's. She actively looked for something positive in her daughter to counteract the negative that had been so easy to pinpoint. Once she saw her daughter taking responsibility and trying to do the right things for the baby's sake, she apologized for her judgments. In future conversations, she resisted her impulse to lecture her daughter, and instead asked how she was doing, if she was having morning sickness or needed anything.

Building Relationship During Difficult Times

Just as Liz, I, and countless other moms have discovered, life has a way of going in a drastically different route than we'd planned. When it does, our thoughts rarely go to the opportunity inherent in the situation. But the Chinese symbol for *crisis* is the same as the word for *opportunity.* Literally translated it reads, "Crisis is an opportunity riding the dangerous wind."

Those dangerous winds come as crisis crashes through: when a daughter encounters a serious health problem, a crisis pregnancy, infertility, addiction, divorce, and so on. The problems and crises are inevitable, but if we can gain perspective of the possibilities, we'll find that each one is an opportunity to grow in our relationship, to support her growing autonomy, and to move us from child-mother to co-adults and true friends.

Help is needed when our daughter has had an accident or lost her job and her unemployment checks have run out. Kindness is important when her heart is broken or she's so down in the dumps she doesn't see any hope ahead. Our friend Kathryn calls it "saturation" when there's a "now need"— when her close friend has died, her fiancé broke the engagement, or she's experienced a miscarriage or the death of a child. These are times when your loving presence will mean the world to your daughter. This doesn't necessarily mean bailing her out but offering love and acceptance.

"What's saturation?" I asked Kathryn.

"It's a lot of listening not talking, bringing dinner and being with her," she explained. "It's being physically close and present, weeping with your daughter, being available, and feeling the pain together. Sitting with her in the midst of unresolved questions so she doesn't feel so alone— that's what communicates acceptance and validation of her loss. You don't have to solve the mystery or come up with 'the answer.' There may not be one at that very moment."

We want to resolve all our daughters' problems, but we can't. Acceptance is something we can teach by our actions and by being willing to sit with them in the pain. If we can model this acceptance rather than having to resolve things, our daughters will learn they are loved, supported, and believed in.

But even in a crisis, it's important not to rescue our adult daughters from their own responsibilities. When we rescue, start making decisions for a daughter, or do her thinking for her, it's what's called "enabling." That's when we try to speak for her and solve her problems for her, especially when that means removing or smoothing over the consequences of destructive behavior and choices.

We can't fix everything in our daughter's tumultuous life or protect her from her own self-destructive behavior. But it is still important to speak the truth. Whether it's a deadly eating disorder, an addiction, a health problem such as diabetes she's not addressing, or an abusive boyfriend, we aren't to judge a daughter's heart or solve her problems. It is not wrong for a mom to question (without attacking) a daughter's actions if they are destructive. The key is to confront the issue without attacking her and draw a boundary so that her destructive patterns don't negatively affect your life.

For instance, you might say something like:

- "When you're willing to get help for yourself, I'll work with you to find it and support you in that."
- "I won't jump on the denial boat with you. I can't stand by and pretend your choices don't concern me, because they do."
- "I love you but I cannot support your destructive behavior, not financially or any other way."

These are not magical words; they may not change her behavior and probably will not. But you can still speak the truth in love and let her know where you stand. It's more important to your sanity and peace of mind to know that you've spoken from your heart and at least it's out there—or in there, if she was listening.

If your daughter can't get unstuck or if things are getting worse, seek professional help from a reputable family service agency or licensed counselor in your area. It's best for us to not try to serve as our daughter's therapist. In any highly emotional or disturbing situation, professional counselors can help develop a workable plan or treatment. You can also go to Al-Anon or find a healthy support group. In other, more extreme crises, such as when a daughter is mugged, raped, or has an abortion, the mom needs serious support. A daughter needs a safe place to land and ongoing support when in crisis, and you will be better equipped to be there for her if you also have support.

Whatever happens, keep building the relationship with your daughter through doing things you can enjoy. One of the best ways to do this is to meet on neutral ground, like my friend Robin did when her daughter was struggling with addiction and life in general. The harder Robin and her husband had tried to rein Marcie in during her adolescence, the harder she pulled away. So when Marcie was nineteen, they decided to let go and let her make her own mistakes and learn from them. And that she did. She married at nineteen and moved to Paris. The marriage fell apart a short time later, and she came back, found an apartment, went back to college, and got a job. Things were still rocky.

"In my twenties I was still completely self-involved and immature, living for myself. It was *all about me.* I was strong-willed and needed to experience life and wasn't going to just have someone tell me about it," Marcie said. "But my parents had stepped back and let me grow up and be myself and make horrible mistakes and loved me through them. They didn't question me. Yet they were there when I asked for advice or help."

Just because Robin wanted to stay connected to her daughter, they met once a week at the mall and had dinner and went to a movie. They walked around and window-shopped, had some "shopping therapy," or stopped and talked awhile. Robin made a point not to bring up anything about the past or her daughter's addiction or problems. Marcie eventually became sober when she was in a second marriage and expecting her first baby. (There's something about those babies!) She's been in recovery for five years from everything, but it was an individual journey, hers and not her parents, even though they have an effective, statewide outreach ministry to those affected by alcoholism and addiction. Later, on her own timetable, she joined Celebrate Recovery in Texas and found having a community was a great ongoing support for her.

Marcie is now in her late thirties, and those connecting times have held her and her mother through the seasons. "We do a lot of laughing—my mom and I," Marcie told me. "I have more fun laughing with her than with any of my friends. We go to movies, and we're going on a trip to California together this summer—just the two of us."

Often what we think is a crisis is actually an opportunity—to love, accept, connect, and believe in our daughters, and to be still and trust God.

A Daughter's Perspective

It was spring, almost midnight, and I was sitting on our brick porch having a glass of wine and a smoke—two things I would anxiously wait for after getting the boys to bed. I hadn't always been a smoker, hadn't always been a drinker, but tonight I was. And many other nights before and after I was; I was alone and afraid and restless and lost. My marriage was in shambles. I was hurting but too ashamed to ask for help. I couldn't control what was going on, couldn't make sense of it, just had to keep living it…day after brokenhearted day.

I felt as if this heartache would never go away. I felt the world was cold and mean with silence and didn't care to wrap its arms around me. It only enveloped me with its darkness. I also felt that I was letting my family down, especially my mom. I unknowingly compared myself to her and resented her for staying so long in a marriage with heartaches but never talking about how that made her feel. So I held it in, drank my way through my disappointment and pain, and felt like a failure. I wanted to know that my mom didn't view me as any less of a person or a failure if my marriage didn't work out. I wanted to know that she identified or empathized with me.

What she did do was make herself available for my many moods and meltdowns in terms of listening, taking us to dinner, and watching the boys so I could get mental health breaks. My mom was sensitive in her words with me during this time. She didn't advise me to death, and she affirmed my marriage by her support for both me *and* Hans too, acknowledging that she was aware of how complex the situation was and that she didn't have any answers. She stayed as neutral as she could. She gave us love and acceptance. Somehow she instinctively knew that I needed her to still love Hans even if I couldn't for a while. But as I would express myself more, I knew she would support me either way our marriage turned out because she told me through the roughest months, "I love you no matter what, and I love you and Hans no matter what."

As we've shared, when I was an early twenty-something, I had existed in an undiagnosed bipolar funk. I was higher than a kite or lower than low. Mostly on the low side was when my mom didn't know what in heaven's name to do with me. I felt that she wanted to make me happy or wave a wand and snap me out of the dark place I was in emotionally. When my marriage and life got harder, I felt that my unhappiness and all my quarter-life crisis angst was doing my mom in. Along with the other stresses going on in her life, she was worried and sad when she couldn't change the way I felt. As our unhealthy, codependent patterns ensued, I became even more depressed that I couldn't alter my moods upon will or get my life together. Our family didn't talk about that stuff; mental things like depression and manic feelings were all hidden.

So my crisis that started out with manic depression turned into trying to self-medicate to appear more "normal" to my family and friends. I drank to suppress the intense feelings, whether up or down. Drinking made me conversational when I wasn't. I hid what I was doing, but the truth was, I could small talk and shoot the breeze and relax, so I thought the drinking was a good addition because I could function more "normally." But chemically and genetically I became addicted to my own prescriptions, and so in the long run, self-medicating only brought on a bigger nightmare. What I was fighting to control but failing at was actually Mom's worst nightmare (alcoholism) and one that she was in denial about for a long time.

At times I wanted to tell her how hard it was to not drink during the day or to fess up to some of my erratic behaviors, but I didn't think she'd understand and so I couldn't talk about it with her.

Finally, I realized that regardless of what my mom or dad or family thought, I had to choose to get help my way. I wasn't going to keep it all hidden like I had seen people do in my family. I needed my mom to embrace reality and to be willing to meet me there and to face her own fears in the process.

We daughters need you to know there is no formula to our pain. We need your patience and kindness while we are struggling or in a crisis. We need your forgiveness, even when we're in a self-made crisis. Please don't hold it against us. Please don't rescue us or do for us what we can do for ourselves. Please don't be desperate for us to "get it." Give us the time we need to grow and learn from life, and please just be with us in the crisis, but don't try to fix us or even fix it, whatever "it" is. We need your respect, even when we haven't arrived and don't make all the choices you might make.

We might be grieving or brokenhearted, the love of our life may have left us, or perhaps we've endured a loss or tragedy. Please don't produce an answer or easy solution for us. If you can be okay with the sound of silence and give us some space to grieve, we will heal…in our own time. Meals are nice, taking us to coffee or a movie and not forcing conversation, such acts of kindness help. If we have children, it helps us if you offer to baby-sit now and then. We need you to love them well. That crisis wasn't the only one.

Very recently, during the time Mom and I were in the midst of rewrites for this book, I endured a crisis totally out of my control. My husband was in the best shape of his life, had been training for the tactical team on the police force, and was a personal trainer on the side. He was struck all at once with a toxic group A strep infection that attacked his heart, lungs, and kidneys. I'd never seen him sick with anything other than a cold and a bout with kidney stones. This superbug hit him hard and fast, and his pulmonologist told us once he was out of critical condition that he was lucky to be alive and still have all his limbs. It was so scary and so close.

This particular strain of strep advances so quickly that in a few days many victims lose arms or legs or their life if treatment is too late. If we hadn't gone that day to the emergency room, it would have been much worse. I remember going into shock when it all happened. I became so fearful of even the thought of losing Hans and wanted to be his advocate at the hospital every second of every day that he was there, but I had two healthy, school-age boys at home.

Who was going to take them to school? Who was going to keep things normal for them? I was a mess of emotions—needing to be with Hans, especially during the critical days, and feeling guilty for not being there for the boys. What eased this dilemma the most was the way my mom went into this amazing gear, kind of supergrandma mode. She didn't ask a lot of questions; she told me simply the boys were being well cared for and not to worry. She kept things going for them with school and soccer, and she kept their spirits up with her Nandy-ability to do so. With the help of her and my mother-in-law, I was able to be 100 percent with Hans for six days and also have total peace about how the boys were doing.

I can't put words on the gift Mom gave me during that crisis time. It bonded me to her in a way I didn't know was possible, because she just did what she knew would free me up the most to care for Hans. I know a part of her wanted to be at the hospital supporting me, making sure Hans and I were okay. But when I expressed to her how loved and at peace I was that the boys were with her night and day, she knew that was the best way to help. Hans was left with pneumonia and some other postinfection issues, though not long-term, and faced weeks of recovery. We all had a greater appreciation for each other as the ordeal passed.

Nothing has the potential to bond us, mother and daughter, like crisis.

But in the fray of it, we need your patience. Will you be okay in living in the unresolved issues with us for a while? Maybe we can even bond there. We daughters have to learn how to function in crises in our own adult lives, and we might fail in the process. Can you accept that?

Crisis already makes everyone's feelings heightened. We need you to know that we might need an extra grace in whatever crisis we are in. We need grace for the way we communicate about it, for our need for distance, or for our need to have you physically closer to help us through. Sometimes we have trouble saying what we need, and it comes out all wrong. Please be patient and don't jump to angry conclusions about our choices that might have led us to where we are. Please don't tell us what we ought to be doing. We need you to be empathetic but honest, not from a teacher standpoint, but like a close friend would be.

Sure, it might be a crisis that you'd never want to happen, but it just might be the tipping point that gets us out of ourselves so that we can mature and connect in a way that you can't plan or manufacture. We become grateful for you in a new way during crisis times. And we learn how to walk through them by seeing your response to them.

Two-Part Harmony

During one of Ali's crisis times, I placed one of my favorite framed photographs of her on the kitchen counter, where I could see it often. In the picture, she was on a trip to Chicago and she was smiling in a genuinely joyful, contented way. I've kept it there for many years—in times when she was depressed or struggling with life. Every time I look at it, it's been a sign of hope and remembering who she really is. In the last few years, she has been becoming the woman she was always meant to be, and it gives me great joy because I know the journey she's taken.

When we moms handle our daughters' crises with patience, remaining optimistic without denying reality, when we avoid blaming others for problems but deal with them and are willing to look at our part, we help our daughters. When we avoid being critical or hostile, but instead have open communication, it contributes to growth in our relationship.

If in the midst of the problems, you experience insomnia, lack of appetite, depression or anxiety, *take care of yourself.* We suggest ways to do that in the next chapter. When we seek help and become good stress managers, we are demonstrating valuable tools a daughter can use when a bolt out of the blue hits her own family. There is so much your daughter can learn from you as you come alongside her and she watches how you handle life's problems. Saturate her with your unconditional love, and she will feel it. It will give her strength even if she might not say it…yet. Even when you don't realize it, she is learning from you how to care for someone in pain or crisis.

Maybe your daughter can't say it right now, but Ali does on her behalf: "Moms, we are grateful for you. We value your life, your experience, your words. But most of all we value your presence in our pain."

As you apply some of the principles in this chapter and throughout the book, we think that as you look back on the experience, you'll find that the very *crisis* that once posed danger, stress, or heartache became an *opportunity* to build an even stronger, more honest and loving relationship with your daughter.

TAKING CARE OF YOURSELF

One great gift a mother can give her daughter
is to live her own life as well as possible.
—HARRIET LERNER, *THE MOTHER DANCE*

As mothers, we often don't major on taking care of ourselves well. There are simply too many people who need us. We sacrifice for others without thinking about it. "Isn't that what mothering is all about—making sacrifices for those kids you love?" one woman asked me. And when our children begin to leave home, we may be the caretaker for aging parents, serve on several committees at church, and volunteer in the community, plus embark on grandparenting. There are so many things to do, and if only there were more hours in the day, we'd get even more accomplished. We focus on taking care of others while putting ourselves on the back burner. We're often the most stressed-out, tired member of the family.

Sound familiar?

When Ali and I talked about this chapter, I asked her for input about what she thought ought to be included, and she said: "Well, you could talk about how moms let themselves go. Like how you didn't take care of yourself during those years that Dad was depressed and you were raising us and carrying the load."

I didn't like that answer. "But I didn't let myself go, Ali. I put on makeup every morning and wore lipstick…" I quickly defended myself and didn't let her finish her sentence.

"But, Mom, we all let ourselves go when we're raising kids; even I do when I don't have enough time."

"Well, I exercised, did my hair, and tried to wear cute clothes. I'm not the fashion queen, but I wanted to look nice—"

"Oh Mom, there you go again," she bristled with annoyance. "You're taking this personally when really I was just trying to say that there were times I worried about you. Especially when you weren't taking care of yourself."

At first I didn't understand what she meant. Did she think I looked like "Granola Mom," as my friend Cynthia's kids described her? Or is it that I resist all her efforts to "update Mom"? But then I realized maybe the real issue for Ali was more than hair and makeup. It was even beyond mammograms and pap smears and taking my calcium (as important as those are, I sometimes forgot them when I was getting the kids' teeth straightened and going to Ali's cross-country races and the boys' tennis matches, basketball, and baseball games). I'd neglected some vital soul care until I was just about at the end of my rope.

Ali wasn't alone in her concern for her mother—lots of daughters expressed this when we interviewed them. Whether they have just left home or moved out years ago, daughters worry about their moms' well-being. If we're in the habit of taking care of everyone but ourselves, or if we're emotionally fragile or depressed, burned out, and exhausted, in ill health, unhappy in our marriage, or just plain lonely, our daughters tend to get anxious about us.

WHAT DAUGHTERS SAY ABOUT THEIR MOMS

While researching and writing this book, we heard daughters of all ages say things like:

- "I'm so glad when my mother works out and takes care of herself. I encourage her in doing it."
- "I worried about my mom when Dad divorced her and she was in the pits. She isolated herself; she didn't go out with friends but stayed at home feeling sorry for herself."
- "After my mother was diagnosed with diabetes, I was constantly concerned for her. She was eating too many carbs, being sedentary, and just kept taking care of Dad and ignoring her own needs like always."
- "My mom started drinking after Dad died. When I got married and moved across the country, I was constantly afraid I was going to get a call that she'd hurt herself or someone else in a car wreck."
- "Since my mom's illness, I'm very protective of her. I call her my "little, little mother," because I'm taller than she is and she seems fragile. If we travel, I drive and carry her bags. I want her to be careful and not overdo."

While I hear some real concern and love in these women's comments, there's another issue. Our daughters want to know we're going *to be okay without them,* so they can move forward with their own lives. Worrying about Mom drains their energy and makes them feel guilty they aren't doing more to help or that they're selfish to build life apart from their mother. The anxiety they feel can even derail their efforts to leave the nest.

That was the case with a young woman I know who left for an out-of-state college with great hopes and lots of enthusiasm. After a few weeks she became so depressed and anxious, she called her parents to come get her. "I've made a mistake. This isn't the college I want to attend. I want to come home," she told them. Her mom was puzzled about what had caused her daughter to bail out. After all, they'd visited numerous college campuses and filled out applications, and this was her pick. They knew she had a health issue that needed treatment, but that wasn't the whole reason.

This bright young woman spent the next two semesters living with her parents and working at her dad's office. All her friends were off at college so she missed those relationships. But the next fall she went to a university an hour away from home. Before she left, she and her mom had a conversation that revealed an underlying worry she'd had all along: "Mom, *are you going to be all right after I'm gone?*" asked this sensitive and caring last child to leave home.

By this time, her mom had resolved some medical and hormonal issues and was in a much better place. She was involved in a community project, had adjusted to their cross-country move, and made some close friends. Mom was happy her daughter had chosen to give college life another try, and she was able to listen to how concerned her daughter had been for her the year before. She assured her she'd be fine, and this time her daughter knew it was true. As a result, she was freer to get involved at the university and not be anxious about how her mother was doing.

PUTTING MYSELF ON THE LIST

I remember one day when Oprah was talking about her battle with weight, and she said, "I'm putting myself on my to-do list." I was struck by Oprah's comment, because as I've looked at my old to-do lists and sticky notes (my favorite organizational tool), I don't see my name on them often. I see lots of tasks, errands, deadlines to meet, and other-oriented activities, which are great. But when life gets hectic, I'm the first thing I drop.

One of the greatest gifts we can give our adult daughters is to put ourselves on our to-do lists. When we do take care of ourselves, the relationship benefits because we're *decreasing* our daughter's guilt and *increasing* healthy connections between mother and daughter. But how do we do that when we're out of practice?

The conversation with Ali I described at the start of this chapter got me thinking about the situation I was in ten years ago. Ali was living with us, and both she and her dad were in an extended funk for several months. I tried everything—encouraging them, sharing hopeful verses, cooking meals, and praying my heart out for them, but nothing changed, at least in them. All my efforts only made them irritated with me and caused them to withdraw even more. One day it hit me—of course I can't change them; I'm not that powerful. I can only change myself, be willing to let God change me, and I needed to get on with it.

Hmm, I thought. Could it be that as long as I was preoccupied with their problems, I didn't have to pay attention to my own?

Once I got quiet enough to ponder this question, I realized how exhausted I was, physically, mentally, and spiritually, and how I had focused all my attention on two people who were severely depressed and miserable. Yet like a hamster running on a never-ending wheel, I didn't know how to break out of the overload syndrome. My husband was working, but the only position he could find paid a part-time salary for full-time work. That put even more pressure on me to work harder. While going on adrenaline a lot of the time, I developed chronic rapid heartbeat.

After my family doctor referred me to a cardiologist, and a stress test and EKG showed my heart was normal, he concluded I was experiencing

what he called "adrenaline dump" from too much adrenaline in my system. That's why when I laid down or tried to relax, my heart raced, and
I'd be unable to go to sleep. Unfortunately, I didn't have the luxury of taking a break for three months, which was his first suggestion. But I did follow the other suggestions, like adding extra days of exercise-walking so my
heart would handle the adrenaline better and resting in the evenings instead of working until midnight.

I also realized that I needed to address some internal issues, particularly why I was so driven and couldn't seem to stop. I wanted to go for
three days of intensive counseling in the Dallas area, but thoughts
popped up. *Aren't we supposed to keep giving and giving and giving—
God first, others second, me last? How can I possibly spend this much money
on myself?* The problem was, if I didn't do something, there wasn't going
to be anymore *me* around to take care of anyone. It was then—when I
shifted my attention to myself—that my own healing journey began.

Nourishing My Emotional Well-Being

I saved enough money for the counseling, not to fix my daughter or my
marriage, which needed a lot of help—but to take a long look at *myself*.
What I discovered in those sessions led me to join a weekly women's support group led by two wise counselors in our city. The journey involved
facing my own issues, my family of origin, and a lot of soul-searching. But
I was beginning to care for myself—from the inside out—and that eventually led to better emotional health.

I wasn't all fixed up in a few months. We never truly *arrive*, but I
sensed that Ali breathed a sigh of relief when she saw me making some
small internal changes, such as obsessing less about her problems and paying more attention to mine, and getting help for addressing issues in my
own marriage.

The external self-care continued to slowly progress: I still worked, of course, but I was more consistent about exercise, I began strength-training, and I got together with three other friends for birthday lunches and long talks. I returned to playing my favorite sport, tennis, on Friday mornings, and this gives me a lot of joy, sunshine, and fresh air. I even take myself to the movies in the middle of the afternoon sometimes—Ali was shocked and thrilled when I told her. And a few summers ago, two lifelong girlfriends and I took a trip to the coast of Maine for a week to celebrate our forty years of friendship.

I discovered along the way that I can't depend on my husband, daughter, or sons for my happiness, even though I love them very much. I found that *I'm* responsible for my own happiness, but joy can be mine if I look in the right places: from a more intimate connection with God and quality time to with him, which brings strength (see Nehemiah 8:10), to spending time doing things I love, such as gardening, playing my guitar, and taking my grandkids to the zoo and park. I'm revived by being outside and riding my bike or by walking on a new urban trail at the park. I love to sit at a patio restaurant at Lake Hefner and watch the brilliant colors of the sunset. Making time for these personal joy fillers makes all the difference in my life.

Once I was listening, more guidance came through Patty Johnston, my mentor and longtime friend. (How kind of God to bring Patty into my life since he knew my own mother would be heading for heaven early, at only fifty-nine years old.) One day I asked Patty the secret of how she's done all the things she did over the years of her forties, fifties, sixties, and beyond. How she handled the running of a successful health food store and restaurant, raised her nephew besides her two daughters, ministered to countless people, and was a great wife and life partner to her husband, Jack, until his death. How she helped found and has championed World Neighbors, an international nonprofit that has helped thousands of people in third-world countries, and helped care for a daughter in her last years of progressive illness. Yet here she was, a vibrant, energetic, and sharp woman in her eighties.

"Surely you've got a secret, and I'd love to hear it," I said.

"Here it is, Cheri. For years, I've taken one day off every single week—*just for me.*"

I had a hard time processing the idea at first. "Just for *you*?" I asked. "Whatever do you do all that day?"

"I don't work that day. I do whatever I please *for myself,* not for anyone else, something that I'd really enjoy taking time for," Patty explained. One week it might be a facial and massage, another it might be a quiet retreat day to listen to the Spirit, or to have lunch out with her daughter or spend the day on her patio reading a book she was fascinated with.

Whatever nourishes her soul, gives her a break—that day is a mini-vacation each week for Patty. That's her secret. Along with yoga and exercise classes; natural, organic food and supplements; meditation; and a rich intellectual life, it's the key to how she's gotten through both good and very difficult years with enough energy for helping a family member or loved one in a crisis. Patty's wisdom has impacted my life, but from a daughter's perspective, her actions have spoken louder than words. I can't take off three months as the doctor recommended, but I can take a day off every week.

MOVING MY BODY

Besides paying attention to our emotional well-being and spending time with friends, one of the things I've learned most about self-care is to keep moving my body. I know it's hard finding time for exercise in the midst of workdays and other responsibilities, even when our kids are gone. But staying consistent with this has helped me survive and keep my energy up for living, writing, teaching, and nowadays being a grandmother.

For the last twenty years I've been a walker. Two years ago I started doing strength training at Curves and was awarded my 200 Days T-shirt. I'm motivated by being around other women, not having to set the machines because it's a computer-programmed circuit. Hearing the fast "Mamma Mia" or other great music CDs keeps me going around the circuit. Do I always have time? No, but I do it anyway.

I encourage you to move your body as well. Find an exercise you enjoy and keep at it. Get a partner if you need one. Use an iPod with your favorite music downloaded onto it, and pick up the pace when you walk your dog. A physician who specializes in stress management said that God, knowing we would live in a stressful world, gave us three terrific antidotes: music, nature, and laughter. Engaging in these pursuits can fill your life with energy and fun.

Try tap-dancing, kickboxing, indoor rock climbing, or racquetball. Once you find what works for you, keep it up. The benefits will amaze you—you'll have more emotional resilience, better muscle tone, and may lose some of those menopause pounds. And maybe you'll even inspire your own daughter to move her body and take care of herself too.

A Daughter's Perspective

I appreciate the way my mom has valued health and fitness and balance. As a kid I remember her playing tennis on a regular basis and her tan skin and trim frame. I remember her dressing up in plaids and pantsuits for teaching and conferences and keeping her hair permed appropriately for the 1980s. I remember how my dad loved getting her a purse for her birthday every year, and so whenever we would go anywhere the smell of fresh, clean leather that matched Mom's penny loafers would accompany us. I was proud that she could jump on skis at Crested Butte and shoot baskets with my brothers. I have a vivid memory of going to my brothers' baseball games, eating orange slices, and feeling I wanted to be like Mom when I grew up. It was one of my favorite things about her. She took care of herself in this way so well.

But even though Mom kept herself healthy and intact physically, she had a harder time valuing her emotional life, and this was hard for me to watch. When my dad and I were simultaneously struggling through years of off-and-on clinical depression and addiction, my mom lost herself in trying to fix us, trying to make us happy. When I was mad or sad, she was trying hard either to deny the reality that it was miserable for her to have such a "down" daughter or to cheer me up.

In reality, she couldn't change me; she couldn't shake the blues or the drinking away from me. I needed to take responsibility for myself, and she needed to take care of herself and keep on living. What I most wanted was for her to still have a life, whether or not I was okay. I wanted for her to do things with friends and to have fun unapologetically. I wished she could sleep in without having to apologize for it, afraid of appearing unproductive if she did. Some of that mind-set was probably ingrained in her from her mom, but to me, if we need sleep, then sleep!

I want my mom to experience the joys in life, no matter what frame of mind I or anyone in our family is in. That must be easier said than done. But it's what I've wanted for her for a long time.

I sensed in my early twenties that Mom's health was shaken from overwork and that she needed a break. It took her a lot of years and a doctor's orders to finally take one. That break was our trip to Europe together, and it was *such* a relief to see her relax, laugh, drink a little wine, not work, and get some distance from all the stress that was going on at home. I loved seeing her relax. Her fun side emerged on that trip, and I didn't have to worry about her so much. She seemed alive and enjoying herself, not trying to make anyone else enjoy life. She wasn't trying to fix anything, she was sitting and reading and not apologizing for chilling out. I love seeing my mom sit. That simple action gives me some peace that she's caring for herself.

My friend Ashley told me about how her mom cares for others so much that it's a detriment to her health. She developed high blood pressure and gained weight. When Ashley and her husband got her mom a full-day gift certificate to a spa as a birthday present, her mom didn't use it, so it expired. It really bothered Ashley. Her mom was so busy helping others she couldn't even receive a gift and take a day for herself.

I think this is an extremely common feeling among daughters. What we want most of all is for you to be happy. We want you to feel the freedom to keep finding yourself, to find your bliss, and to value yourself enough to take care of yourself, whatever that means for you. We want you to find life as being full and joyful, with or without us, just because you value yourself enough to.

When I asked a few daughters of various ages, "What does it feel like when your mom takes care of herself?" I heard the following responses:

- "I don't have to worry about her physically and emotionally."
- "I'm proud of her and want to be like her when I have my own kids, careful to take the time I need to feel sane."
- "It feels like she's got her own life, and I'm not her only friend."
- "It feels like a relief, peace of mind, and it makes me happy when she's happy apart from me."

When I asked the opposite question, "What does it feel like when your mom doesn't take care of herself?" I received answers like these:

- "I worry about her and her health."
- "I feel sorry for her and that she isn't enjoying life more."
- "I wish she wasn't so afraid of change and she'd get out of that rut."

- "I feel like I don't want to hang out with her as much because she doesn't seem happy or satisfied and I can't make her happy."
- "I wish she knew how much everyone loved her and she would stop feeling like they don't."

Can you hear the longing in our voices for you to "put yourself on the list" and care for your own needs? We really want you to because we love you.

Two-Part Harmony

Since Ali now has children, she sees how much work it is to put the oxygen mask on herself first before she puts it on those she loves—like the flight attendants say upon takeoff. It's hard to prioritize self-care, both internal and external. But we've both learned the hard way how important it is, because if we don't take care of ourselves, we'll make life miserable for those who love us the most, or they may start having to take care of *us*.

When we take care of our bodies and our hearts, our daughters love it. And when we engage in activities that refresh us or lifestyle changes that contribute to better health or get medical help or counseling when we need it, it teaches our daughters some valuable principles: that it's not okay to take care of others to our own detriment. We can value ourselves enough to change something or get help in order to do so.

Daughters are saying: *Please Mom, take care of yourself.* They really value you and want you to value yourself enough to take that plunge and be a little selfish. Ask for help if you need it. Go on a trip and don't feel guilty. Show your daughter that it's okay to take a little time for yourself by letting her see you be good to yourself.

The Power of
Forgiveness

• • • • •

*As we practice the work of forgiveness we discover
more and more that forgiveness and healing are one.*
—Agnes Sanford

• • • • •

I n the movie *Because I Said So,* Diane Keaton plays Daphne, a
divorced yet overprotective mother of three adult daughters,
who has a tendency to micromanage their lives. Two of them are married,
but because Milly, her youngest daughter, has muddled through a number of failed relationships and breakups, Daphne decides it's time to intervene in her life. Out of fear that Milly is going to turn out as alone as
she is, Daphne puts a personal ad on the Internet with a list of qualities
she's looking for in the perfect husband for Milly. She interviews a large
number of young men, and what results is a romantic triangle that fuels
the plot.

When Milly finds out about the personal ad, she thinks her mother
selected the two guys she's dating, and she's furious. For days they don't
speak, and Milly stays holed up in her house not answering the phone,
especially when it's her mother.

"Please pick up, Milly. It's been four days," she hears Daphne say one night on the phone message.

On another call Mom tells her she found the recipe for the Italian cake her grandmother made on her third birthday. She's tempted but doesn't pick up, and we can hear the sadness in her mother's voice as she hangs up.

The next few calls are attempts at reconciliation and advice giving "I've learned my lesson, because Milly, it's your life…" Still no reply from her daughter. It is really, really hard for this mom to put aside her pride and admit she is wrong, but finally the distance between them is just too painful, and she calls Milly again, this time ready to be honest and ready to apologize.

As she gazes at the black-and-white photograph of herself as a young mother holding her baby daughter, she tearfully says, "Milly, I never meant to hurt you, sweetie. And I promise I will never, ever interfere ever again. I was only… I guess what I'm trying to say is that I was just trying to protect you from becoming me."

Finally, Milly picks up—"Mom?"

"Hi, honey."

"I miss you."

"I miss you too."[1]

What I like about this story is how it shows the restorative power of asking for forgiveness. This mother made numerous calls in an attempt to get her daughter to speak to her again, but not until she took a long, hard look at herself and sincerely apologized did her daughter's heart open to her.

Although we can't force our daughters to forgive us and while for-giveness can't be forced, restoration becomes much more likely when we moms are humble enough to admit our part in a misunderstanding or hurt. You see, when a relationship with a daughter is broken, it means the daughter has been hurt, whether Mom intended to hurt her or not. Before the relationship can heal and begin to be restored, *Mom* needs to reach out to her daughter and ask forgiveness.

In order for this to be real and believable, Mom needs to look at herself honestly and acknowledge how she failed her daughter in some way. Only from that place can the request for forgiveness ring true. Otherwise the daughter won't buy it, and her resentment toward her mom will continue to build. It never works to demand or "guilt" someone into forgiveness. Of course, even when you admit your mistakes and failures and ask for forgiveness, your daughter may not be in a place to extend grace at that moment. Forgiveness takes time, so be patient and offer grace.

THE POWER OF FORGIVENESS

Since the mother-daughter relationship is one of the most intimate of all human relationships, it has the potential for conflict. "The closer the relationship, the more conflict," says counselor Ruthie Hast, M.Ed., LPC. Just as Daphne did, we do things that anger our daughters or motivate them to distance themselves from us, even though we think we are trying to help them or make their lives better.

It's easy to think, *I haven't done anything but be good to her. Why's she mad at me?* We think our daughter is just touchy or difficult to get along with. But when we look at what we may have done to cause the rift, it can lead to healing and reconciliation.

I've discovered the power of forgiveness in my relationship with Ali. Three years ago I walked through the double doors of Valley Hope Treatment Center in Grapevine, Texas, a place I never thought I'd be visiting my daughter. I was struck by the drabness of the building. *This is no fancy Betty Ford rehab resort,* I thought. I stopped at the front desk to ask the receptionist where Ali might be.

"They're at break now. You'll probably find her somewhere on the patio or in her room," the woman said and pointed down to the nurses' station. As I walked down a long, narrow hallway to find my daughter, I saw a group of guys huddled around a big flat screen TV. Near the coffeepot two women worked on a puzzle. Through the big glass windows I saw a group of men and women outside smoking.

Flashbacks of treatment centers went through my mind. My big sister, Martha, had been in and out of rehab many times before her recovery from alcoholism began. Then I saw a man who looked strangely like my uncle Jarrell, my father's only brother, who died of alcoholism. His addiction not only shortened his life, but on many occasions it also made our whole family miserable, such as the numerous times when my father was called away from dinner to bail out his drunken brother from jail.

I *never* wanted this disease to affect my family. Alcoholism was my worst fear. I cried buckets remembering how scared I was as a kid when inebriated Uncle Jarrell tried to beat down our back door when Papa wasn't home. I had only started facing my fear two years before when I had an intervention for my husband's drinking problem.

Then I saw Ali walking toward me. Hair bunched up in a big clip, she didn't have makeup on; I couldn't have been more glad to see her. I opened my arms and gave her a hug, at that moment, thinking, *A week ago this is not where I thought I'd be visiting my daughter.* She stiffened a bit and there was some awkwardness between us. But as we sat down on a worn, brown leather couch and began to talk, I sensed that this was the place she was supposed to be. She told me about her counselor, Kevin, and that through sessions with him and her chaplain and group therapy, she was learning some things about herself and her addictions.

As Ali told me what was going on, I felt incredibly proud of her for willingly checking herself in for thirty days of treatment. Though I struggled with guilt-laden thoughts, like *How have I failed as a mother and how did my precious daughter wind up here?* the overarching feeling was gratefulness. I sensed how coming to this out-of-state treatment center was perhaps the most difficult thing Ali had ever done. To me she was very courageous for not letting herself continue on the downward path she had been on.

"I'm doing this for the boys," she told me, as tears formed in the corners of her eyes just thinking about them. I knew it was excruciatingly difficult to be away for a whole month from the four- and five-year-old sons she adored.

On the way home I continued to struggle with guilt about what I did or didn't do that led to Ali's alcohol problem. As moms we have the illusion that somehow we're powerful enough to prevent bad things from happening to our kids, and we feel awful when we haven't stopped the damage or when we discover we contributed to it in some way.

A few days later, as the January rain beat on the windows of our small second-floor Dallas apartment, I cried out to God, not only for strength and hope for my daughter but also for me to see *my part* in her addiction. For a long time I sobbed into the carpet, pouring out my sadness at what had happened to my daughter. Then a glimmer of light began to dawn. This tiny bit of clarity didn't make me feel better; in fact, I felt worse.

I saw that in my working and working, I had put my head in the sand. I realized that my previous denial about my husband's secret alcohol problem (and later, my overfocus on how to fix him) had contributed in certain ways to my daughter's problems. Her behavior had mirrored his, and when she needed her dad the most, he had been emotionally unavailable. Though I didn't have control over his addiction or some of the other factors that had affected Ali, I regretted that I didn't have the strength or know-how to get help for our family. Through those mistakes and my optimistic approach that "surely things are going to get better," I'd failed my daughter.

I knew what I had to do. It was still pouring outside, but I got my purse and keys, pulled out the umbrella, and headed for the car. As I drove the forty-five miles to the treatment center, I talked to God all the way, focused not on my daughter's problems but on the great need I had for mercy and forgiveness.

I parked the car by the smoking porch and Ali saw me. She walked over, and I began to tell her about how I regretted my inaction, my denial, and my failure to deal with the reality of her dad's addiction head-on. I talked about my part in our troubled relationship and apologized for my flaws that had hurt her. No excuses, no defending myself, just an "I'm sorry." Ali hugged me and graciously forgave me. It was a moment of release and reconciliation I'll never forget. It hasn't been the only time I've asked her to forgive me in the last few years, but it was a start and our relationship began to rebuild.

WHEN WE'VE HURT OUR DAUGHTER

Because we're all imperfect mothers—despite our best efforts—most of us haven't lived up to our daughters' expectations. Most daughters feel their mothers have disappointed or hurt them at some point—and some of those criticisms are based in the reality of what Mom did wrong. When we realize that a mistake we made in the past has harmed our daughter's life and admit it, it can have enormous healing benefits on the relationship. Two simple words—*I'm sorry*—if sincerely spoken, can bridge the wide gap between a mom and daughter.

MOM AND DAUGHTER RECONCILED

Nancy and her mom had a good relationship until Nancy turned thirteen and her dad separated from her mom. Her mother had been a stay-at-home mom raising five children, three who were grown up and on their own. Mom struggled, and Nancy was angry at the self-pity that enveloped her mother. Nancy was facing a lot of difficulties as a teenager and didn't think her mom even tried to connect with her. It seemed as if all her mom did was cry and feel sorry for herself. So Nancy acted out, and they argued constantly. Finally, at the age of fifteen, Nancy ran away from home to live with her oldest sister in another state. After a while, her sister told Nancy she had to move out on her own because they weren't getting along. Nancy was lonely and broke and finally contacted her mom. Before they got off the phone, her mother said she was praying for her. Nancy lived in Maryland and her mother in Florida.

A number of years went by, and Nancy met and married a young man in Virginia, where she'd later moved. After the birth of her second child, when Nancy was thirty, her mom traveled to her home to meet the new baby.

One afternoon, mother and daughter went shopping with the kids. Before they went into Kohl's, they sat in the car and talked about how sorry they were for things said and done in the past.

"I can remember this like it was yesterday," Nancy told me, "because it had never happened. That day my mom asked me to forgive her for not meeting my needs or listening when I was a teenager, for being so wrapped up in self-pity that she ignored my struggles. I forgave my mom and then asked for forgiveness for the way I behaved as a teenager, and she forgave me. We cried and hugged and had a fabulous day together."

The wonder and miracle of forgiveness is expressed in Nancy's next words: "And from that day forward, Mom and I began relating like friends. We pray for each other and talk often. She and I can talk about anything. I love my mom! She's the most wonderful mother in the world, and I wouldn't trade her for anything. God has blessed me with a great adult relationship with her, and she's been a joy in my children's lives."

Although this mother and daughter hadn't lived near each other or been close for fifteen years, when Mom took responsibility for her shortcomings, their relationship was restored. The wonderful connection they have is making up for the days and years that had been stolen from them by misunderstanding and resentment, and is blessing the next generation as well.

MAKING AMENDS

Let's look at some principles that help us take responsibility and make amends. To make amends means admitting responsibility and making things right and usually involves saying, "I'm sorry." First of all, remember that if there is something you apologize to your daughter about, *it doesn't mean you are a failure as a mother.* None of us are perfect moms; we are flawed in some way. We have difficulties or brokenness in our lives, which sometimes derails us from what we'd like to be for our kids. Worse, those difficulties can inflict damage on our children. I struggled to admit my failures because I'd wanted the best for our kids, and I endeavored to be the best mom I could. When I faced some of the blunders and flaws that affected them, and especially Ali, I felt horrible. I was regretful and wept at my own weaknesses, denial, or thoughtlessness. But after a while, I realized I couldn't stay stuck there—wallowing in failure—because that didn't help anyone. It wasn't operating in what I knew was true—that on the cross Jesus took those sins and failures and would forgive me. All I needed to do was ask for his forgiveness, and he would. When my daughter graciously forgave me as well, the freedom I experienced and the closer relationship we have had as a result—not just of one apology, but walking in ongoing humility and forgiveness with each other—became well worth it.

I can't guarantee your daughter will extend forgiveness to you immediately. Often true reconciliation doesn't happen on our timetable. It is a process, not an overnight experience. It may take time for your daughter to see your sincerity or changed attitude. But reaching out to her is a step in the right direction. When you do, be clear about what you're apologizing for. Take responsibility for specific words or deeds that hurt your daughter. If you can tell she's been angry or resentful, ask her in what ways you've hurt her. Then purpose also to change your behavior so you don't repeat it over and over, making the wounds even deeper. Be aware that bearing a grudge or holding on to resentment toward your daughter hurts your relationship *and* your own emotional health. Is there something you need to forgive her for like disappointing you, lying, or disrespecting you? Going through the process of forgiving her even if she never says "I'm sorry" can breathe fresh air into your own life and your mother-daughter connection. Then having done your part, you can trust the relationship to God.

Trust time. Trust God. Know that you are beginning a chain of healing and restoration, not only in this precious relationship but also in other relationships throughout your family.

A Daughter's Perspective

My mom's asking me for forgiveness was the pivotal moment in our relationship. I didn't learn to apologize to my mom, or anyone, until I went into treatment. Before that time, resentments had built such a wall and I was so attached to my sense of rightness, I couldn't be honest with my mom. I was tired of our frustrating disagreements. I was weary of feeling that both of us wanted to be closer but neither knew how to do it.

Until that day at treatment. When my mom said, "I'm sorry," and meant it without any rationalizing or defending herself, I was moved to do the same, and we had a breakthrough in our relationship. She apologized for specific things she had said, done, or not done. That day we accepted our differences and our humanity, and I was able to see who my mom was for the first time in my adult life. We'd had moments of connection like this but had not been able to leave the past behind.

Up to that point, Mom couldn't seem to let herself off the hook. She even took responsibility for things that had really been my responsibility or failures. I, in turn, mirrored her tendency toward shame and lack of forgiveness of self. I most wanted her to acknowledge her own worth and to claim it with confidence instead of staying stuck in a mode of self-criticism or perfectionism.

So when I witnessed my mom applying forgiveness to me and to herself, my respect for her grew. I saw that she wanted to live life, not just exist in the aftermath of old family crises. I saw that she was brave enough to face her past instead of living in denial, and I was stunned by her courage to deal with it. Her example helped me face my past and take responsibility for the pain I'd caused.

I had plenty to apologize for in terms of the worry I caused her and the disappointment she must have felt when I was distant and resentful toward her. But I didn't know how to ask forgiveness until she showed me how by her own genuine example. Someone once said, "Forgiveness is simply love put into action." When Mom put her love into action, it also opened the door for me to be grateful for her in new ways. I was finally able to feel like the daughter and to stop the cycle of unhealthy role reversal that we'd lived in the past.

When we daughters hear our moms say the words, "I'm sorry," we feel relief, because it says you're willing to see things from our perspective. Most of all, an invitation to forgive feels like a healing balm over our wounds from past experiences. It validates the pain and disappointment we have felt and lets us know that our mother really *sees* us.

When you apologize, it shows us daughters how to do the same with our children, our spouses, and ultimately with you. We are impacted by your words and humility, but mostly by the heart behind the words.

When my mom and I began writing this book, I tried to tell her what to feel, what to remember, and how to see the past and present. The experience of writing helped me see that I would continue the same cycle of codependency and unhealthy worry if I didn't look at my own codependent behaviors and make amends to her. I don't know if I could have done this if she hadn't done her part. It felt so good to make amends to her.

God healing us versus us trying to fix each other feels eternally better. When I released resentment, it made me feel free. We had to wade through a minefield of issues and hurt at times, but it was so worth it to find our own truths, our own feelings, and begin to experience each other rather than try to "fix" each other. Once we were able to talk openly about the past without the zingers and tenseness that would bubble to the surface, we were able to start healing and each become our own person.

All our mother-daughter relationships are so full of twists and turns, closeness and distance, that if we don't admit our own imperfections, closeness eludes us. I know firsthand that when I am stubborn and headstrong and vehemently attached to my "rightness," there is zero growth in my relationship with my mom, or anyone else for that matter.

Forgiveness is one of the most transformative experiences available in relationships. It enabled me to finally give and forgive as a woman to a woman, a daughter to a mother. Forgiveness allowed me to grow up, claim my true self, and allow my mom to claim her true self. I have found peace in forgiveness, both in giving it and asking for it.

Two-Part Harmony

Not long ago Ali and I watched *CBS Sunday Morning* as Patti Davis, author of *The Lives Our Mothers Leave Us: Prominent Women Discuss the Complex, Humorous, and Ultimately Loving Relationships They Have with*

Their Mothers, discussed her stormy relationship with her mother, Nancy Reagan. After decades of conflict and even years of not speaking, this mother and daughter have healed their rift. But it only happened in the latter part of Mrs. Reagan's life.

"It's not like a Hallmark card," Patti Davis remarked to interviewer Lesley Stahl. "We've gone through a lot to get here." Mrs. Reagan admitted that one of the most painful and difficult parts of her life was her daughter's estrangement and their years of misunderstanding and distance. During the time her parents were in the White House, Patti readily acknowledged being "at war" with her mom and dad because her liberal stance and their conservative one clashed. Healing their relationship was a slow and difficult journey.

Mrs. Reagan was gracious and candid as she discussed the pain of their difficult mother-daughter relationship, "Most mothers and daughters go through this experience, this period. However, at the end of the day, they'll probably be back together."[2] Then the program showed the defining moment at her father's funeral service, when Mrs. Reagan collapsed in tears, leaning into her daughter's arms. The affection between them was obvious.

The mother-daughter bond is one of the most crucial and foundational the two of you will ever have; it has the most potential to bring you great joy or intense heartache. I know there will come a day when roles will reverse for Ali and me, and I'll be thankful that our relationship is reconciled and there's no resentment between us. That's why it's worth it to work on our relationship, to own up to our part of misunderstandings, and to know that we can find our own melody and harmonize instead of clashing. And forgiveness is a key part of that process.

EPILOGUE

* * * * *

My mom is a never-ending song in my heart of
comfort, happiness, and being. I may sometimes
forget the words but I always remember the tune.
—GRAYCIE HARMON

* * * * *

While we were working on this book, there were some days where Ali and I weren't understanding each other or not getting along, and I thought, *What are we doing writing a book on mother-daughter relationships?* Well, perhaps that *is* the reason we were writing it, because we've been through difficult times and have come out on the other side as friends.

Ali's and my relationship was doing well when we signed the contract with our publisher, but it is even more restored and peaceful now. While writing this book we entered mother-daughter counseling with Ruthie Hast, a wise and understanding therapist, and we've both grown. Though there were some intense soul-searching and teary moments, we've both had chances to say, "I'm sorry," and enter into the marvelous and mysterious process of forgiveness. As we look back, we are amazed at the threads of hurtful situations from the past that have been tied together and released. We definitely have a more connected, healthy mother-daughter relationship.

Since we've worked on each of the concepts we've shared with you, we now *laugh a lot more together*! That's a big step for us and important in the mother-daughter relationship because, "Laughter is enduring—one could say, immortal. It loosens the seams between life and death. We keep our hold on those who laughed with us, who found life to be great fun; and time does nothing to loosen that hold."[1]

We've learned how to address each other in conflict or misunderstandings instead of stewing about them or overreacting. We apologize if we need to and forgive and move on. We give each other space but know when we need to plan something special or fun—even if that's just a chick flick or dessert at our favorite restaurant—to reconnect when we've both been busy or stressed by the demands of our schedules. Ali has become one of my dearest friends.

By way of update, my husband and I continue in recovery and our relationship is much better. It's always freeing when you get the elephant out of the living room, name the problem for what it is, and talk about where you are as individuals and in your relationships. Then you can battle the issues together, and they don't separate you. Sobriety, counseling, months of working on our marriage and being patient with each other—plus the prayers of dear friends and hefty doses of God's grace—have contributed to our moving from winter to spring in our marriage relationship and helped us have healthier connections in our family. Ali and Hans's marriage is stronger and happier also. How thankful we are.

While Ali and I haven't arrived at some perfect place, we are singing more in tune than we ever have before. We are learning our individual parts. I'm not singing her alto part, and she's not singing my soprano anymore. We are finding our own voices. Sometimes we still get off-key, but as practice makes perfect, we start again and enjoy the beautiful harmonies when we find them.

After reading our book, we hope you'll be inspired that if *we* can become friends after the struggles we've been through, then you can too! The mother-daughter relationship is a personal and complex dynamic, and no two situations are the same. Perhaps you have more than one daughter, and you find yourself singing a different tune with each one. As you read parts of our story as well as stories from other mothers and daughters, you probably saw some of your own story. And though your story is not exactly like ours, we hope you could relate to the common struggle found in many relationships. There's such a rich relationship to be had when you understand and apply the concepts we've shared:

- Learn to let go.
- Try to understand your daughter's needs.
- Believe in your daughter even if she's taking a different path than you wanted for her.
- Respect her and set boundaries for yourself.
- Listening is often the best form of communication.
- Take care of yourself; your daughter actually wants you to.
- Forgiveness is a powerful key to unlocking your daughter's heart.
- Trust God, and trust his love for your daughter.

We hope to have raised your awareness as to how you relate to your adult daughter and how she responds to your words and actions. As you move forward, may that awareness translate into choices that resolve conflict, build lasting and meaningful relationships, and create your unique mother-daughter duet. Remember, patience, love, and grace will get you there. Never give up hope. Even if your daughter isn't ready to sing with you, you can still sing your song and work on your part of the music.

DISCUSSION QUESTIONS

Introduction: An Intricate Duet

1. Describe your relationship with your daughter as it is right now. What parts of the authors' discussion relates to experiences you've had, either with your own mom or one of your daughters?

2. What is your hot button—the issue or situation that may trigger harsh words or hurt? Your daughter's?

3. What would you like to change about your mother-daughter relationship?

4. What frustrates you about the relationship? What are your hopes and fears regarding your connection?

5. What were (or are) *your* major needs when your daughter left home? What feelings did you experience in the first days and weeks of her departure?

Chapter One: Letting Go

1. What is holding you back from letting go of your daughter—emotionally, spiritually, or physically?

2. What were your feelings when you "left the nest" of your parents' home? How did your mom/parents handle your desire to be an independent person?

3. If your daughter is in college or is working and living on her own, what helped you deal with the transition into this new stage or the feelings of loss?

4. Cheri described the addiction her family struggled with that brought codependency and tension into her connection with

her daughter. If anything beyond your control affected your family and mother-daughter relationship, what was that issue? How did it affect the two of you?

5. This chapter discussed things that moms need to let go of in order to release their daughters in a healthy, loving way. What do you need to let go of? Write those things down, and pray about them.

Chapter Two: Generational Differences

1. How is your daughter's generation different from yours? How have those differences created distance or tension between you and your daughter?

2. What unresolved hurt from your mother might you have passed on to your daughter, continuing a cycle of hurt or misunderstanding?

3. What would you have liked your own mother to have said or done differently? Try to do these things with your daughter and forgive your mom for her mistakes and flaws, and you'll go a long way toward a peaceful relationship.

4. How might you approach the issue with your daughter so that it might be healed?

5. What do you admire about your daughter's generation of women? Make a list and share it with a friend and at some point with your daughter.

Chapter Three: Validating Your Daughter

1. As moms, we may become vocal about a daughter's appearance for these reasons:
   • We want her to look her best.
   • We don't like her untraditional, edgy appearance.

- We subconsciously feel she's a reflection of us.
- We're worried about her weight gain (or another issue).
- We have control issues.
- Other:_____

Which one of these might be the root of tension between you and your daughter?

2. What had you imagined or hoped your daughter would look like? How does she match up with that vision?

3. When your identity was emerging and developing and you tried to experiment with different clothes and hairdos, what was your style? Did your mother voice her approval, or did she criticize your look? What about during the rest of your adult life? How did her comments make you feel?

4. One of the best things we can do for our daughters is to take care of our own self-image so we don't project a negative one on them. How is yours? How might you change your approach in order to extend grace, be a good role model, or focus on what really matters? Write down *one step* you can take to do this.

5. How do you feel about and care for your own body? What part of your body do you have the most trouble accepting and being grateful for?

Chapter Four: Too Close for Comfort

1. If you sit back and think about what you wanted *at the age your daughter is,* it could help build understanding and empathy into the framework of your changing relationship. What did you feel at your daughter's current age?

2. What words would you have wanted your mom to say to help you feel empowered and capable of growing up and leaving the nest?

3. What do you want ultimately for your daughter that holding her too close now might inhibit?

4. We've been talking about some of the challenges in our mother-daughter connection. What are the *strengths* in your relationship with your daughter?

Chapter Five: Respect and Belief

1. What was your ideal of what your daughter might be like and be doing at the age she is now? How close is the reality to what you'd hoped or imagined?

2. The Message paraphrases Philippians 4, which contains very good words for mothers of adult daughters: "Summing it all up, friends, I'd say, you'll do best by filling your minds and meditating on things true, noble, reputable, authentic, compelling, gracious—the best, not the worst; the beautiful, not the ugly; things to praise, not things to curse. ... Do that, and God, who makes everything work together, will work you into his most excellent harmonies." Think about:

   • What is best about your daughter?
   • What is beautiful about her?
   • What are some things to praise?

3. Once you begin to focus on the above answers, perhaps with a running list of positives in your journal, then belief and respect in your daughter will grow. Purpose to comment on one when the opportunity arises. As you do, your words and even more your spirit of gratitude and acceptance will bless your daughter.

4. If your daughter seems angry or frustrated with you at times, what may be underneath her feelings?

5. Many of us react rather than respond. If we've been hurt either

in the past or present, we may strike out and hurt those close to us with critical words—including our daughters. Interrupting that reaction starts with deciding how you want to behave toward her. After reading this chapter, what would you like to change about your interaction with her?

Chapter Six: Communication

1. Which of the mother-daughter situations in this chapter do you most identify with?
2. What are your expectations regarding your mother-daughter conversations? What do you hope they'll be like? How do you react when those expectations aren't met?
3. Which of these character qualities do you need to work on to improve your mother-daughter conversations?
   - Attentive listening
   - Being open about your mistakes and flaws
   - Understanding instead of trying to get your daughter to see your point of view or prove your rightness
   - Forgiveness
   - Other:_____
4. What was a time without realizing it that you "bought turkey and grapes" instead of sitting down and emotionally connecting with your daughter? What was her reaction, and why could this become frustrating?
5. What taboo subjects do you need to talk about with your daughter?

Chapter Seven: Connecting and Bonding

1. Do you know what your daughter likes to do for fun, what she enjoys? If not, would you be willing to ask her and talk about it?

2. Start a written inventory of what your daughter likes to do. What does she enjoy apart from work or household tasks that she might consider doing with you? Cooking classes? Shopping? Hiking? Bicycling? Going to concerts or art museums? Or _____

3. What do you enjoy doing for fun? What is a stress reliever for you? Do you give yourself permission to let go of the serious issues or worries and just have fun? If not, how might you change that?

4. Think about what your mom did with you that contributed to your feeling closer to her or more valued. What would you have liked to do with her?

5. What is your language of feeling loved, and what is your daughter's? Do they mesh or clash? Are you willing to speak her love language if it's very different from yours? (For details, see *The Five Love Languages* by Gary Chapman.)

Chapter Eight: Are You Going to Church, Honey?

1. As this chapter suggested, we can calm our anxious thoughts about our daughter's faith or lack of it by remembering how and when God got hold of us. Go back and recall where you were spiritually at the age your daughter is right now. How long did it take God to get through to you? When did you have some kind of spiritual awakening or reconnection with God?

2. In what ways was your own mother a stepping stone or a stumbling block on your spiritual journey?

3. What did God use in your life to get you from there to where you are now spiritually?

4. What can you learn from your own journey to apply in your relationship with your daughter and her spiritual pathway?

5. What are your fears and anxieties about your daughter and her faith? Write out your prayer for your daughter's spiritual growth, and list each fear; then consciously give those to God.

Chapter Nine: When Your Daughter Says, "I Do"

1. What things could you do (or did you do) to help make the engagement and wedding a relationship-building rather than distancing process?

2. What unmet hopes or expectations did you have during your own engagement or wedding day?

3. What could you do to let your daughter's wedding be more about her and not about you and what you want?

4. If your daughter's wedding is in the past, what were some of the wonderful moments or blessings of that event or the time leading up to it you want to remember?

5. How can you help relieve some of your daughter's stress or confusion during this sensitive time? Can you ask her what she needs outside the realm of the wedding and reception?

Chapter Ten: Now That She's a Mom

1. How did you feel and what did you experience as a mother? What were your internal or external struggles? Think about how to apply those reflections to empathizing with what season your daughter is in.

2. If your daughter is a mom, what helped her most that you did for her or the baby? If you haven't yet, ask the new mom what you can do to help her the most. After dialoguing with her about her needs, jot down her responses.

3. What are your needs as grandmother in this changing time?

4. As your daughter has become a mother and has her own family,

what kind of network of support and friends of your own do you have?

5. What do you wish your mom did to help you emotionally or physically when you had kids? What did she do that made all the difference?

6. What do you enjoy about being a grandmother? Do you feel accepted by your daughter and feel that you have access to the grandkids? What are ways you can bond with them and increase the enjoyment factor of this season, whether or not your daughter and you are getting along? Check out Cheri's book *Connect with Your Grandkids: Fun Ways to Bridge the Miles* (Focus/Tyndale, 2009) for some great ideas for building a relationship with grandchildren of all ages.

Chapter Eleven: When Crisis Arises

1. Dig deep; even though it is your daughter in crisis, how do you respond when you feel like it reflects on you? If you struggle with this, talking to a friend or finding a support group like Al-Anon will help you cope.

2. Think back to a crisis in your life. What did a friend or family member do that most helped or comforted so you didn't feel so alone? How can you apply that to your daughter?

3. In what ways have you let your daughter's crisis dictate your own happiness and well-being? What could help you distance yourself in a healthy way, if need be?

4. What are some concrete ways you can deal with stress for yourself or help relieve your daughter's stress level?

5. What might keep you from talking openly and honestly with your daughter about the crisis? What subjects have been "off-

limits" or secrets you or your family have locked in the vault?
How could you be more open and honest if she needs that?

Chapter Twelve: Taking Care of Yourself

1. On a scale of 1 to 10, how well do you think you take care of
   yourself—both internally and externally? What are the positives in your self-care, such as what do you do for yourself—
   exercise, healthy eating, friendship, and so on?

2. How are you meeting your needs for companionship, intimacy,
   and conversation? What do you do for yourself when you are
   stressed?

3. How do you think your daughter sees you in the area of self-
   care? Does she worry about you? Consider asking her opinion
   and jotting it down here.

4. Cheri differentiates between taking care of herself on the outside (hair, clothes, and so on) and the inside, the part we moms
   often neglect because of our busyness and care for others. What
   could you do to take better care of yourself—*body, soul, and
   spirit*? Which of the three do you need to focus on? What is
   one new habit or pattern you could implement that could be
   a first step?

5. Break out of your comfort zone by asking yourself: What activities energize me? What would I like to change? What have
   I always dreamed of doing? What steps would I need to take
   to make my dream a reality?

Chapter Thirteen: The Power of Forgiveness

1. We share in this chapter that forgiveness is a change agent that
   opens hearts and minds to the possibility of living life in a new

way. How could you apply the forgiveness principle to your relationship with your daughter or your own mother?

2. We can't undo the past, but we can take responsibility for our part. As you read this or other chapters, what came to mind that you feel guilt or responsibility for that affected your daughter—perhaps actions, words, or attitude toward her?

3. A change of behavior keeps us from perpetuating wrongs. If there is one change of behavior that would help improve your relationship with your daughter, what would it be?

4. What are the ways your daughter may have let you down, hurt you by critical words, rebellion, or disrespectful actions that you need to forgive her for?

5. Where does God seem to be in your circumstances or relationships? Where is he working in your daughter's?

ACKNOWLEDGMENTS

From Cheri:

Heartfelt thanks, Ali, creative coauthor, for sharing this journey both of writing together and connecting in deeper ways as mom and daughter. I'm so grateful for you and for this opportunity to collaborate with you.

Heartfelt thanks, Alice Crider, our editor at WaterBrook Multnomah, for catching a vision for our book and for all the insights you shared in its development, and for Liz Heaney for bringing your expertise to our writing process. Thanks to the WaterBrook Multnomah team for your efforts and skills in bringing *Mother-Daughter Duet* to life.

Thank you, Catherine Hart Weber, Leslie Vernick, Georgia Shaffer, Debi Stack, and Cynthia Spell Humbert for conversations and insights you shared with me on mother-daughter relationships.

For dear praying friends, I'm immensely grateful for your prayers and encouragement as we wrote and revised: Patty J. Johnston, Janet Page, Kathy Wirth, Cynthia Tonn, Betsy West, Lindsey O'Conner, Carol Hartzog, Peggy Stewart, Glenna Miller, Cynthia Morris, Corrie Sargeant, Susan Stewart, Cathy Herndon, Pam Whitley. Tiffany and Maggie, thanks for your sweet calls, prayers, and inspiration and for being a blessing in my life.

Thank you, Mimi, for being such a marvelous role model of a loving mom, grandma, and mother-in-law. And I'm thankful for my mom, long ago graduated to heaven; thank you for all the prayers, birthday parties, handmade pinafores, and loving us in a million ways.

Ruthie Hast, how grateful I am for your understanding, insightful questions, and counseling with Ali and me as we journeyed to more wholeness and harmony in our relationship, and how God used you to bring new areas of healing and freedom in my life. To Robin and Jim Riley, you have been a blessing to Holmes and me and our family in countless ways, and we're immensely grateful to you and the Outreach as you've come alongside us in this recovery journey.

I'm very grateful all those moms and daughters who were willing for us to interview you. Thanks for your honesty and sharing your stories.

Most of all, thank you, Maggie, Tiff, Justin, Chris, and Hans for your encouragement, and Holmes, for your willingness for us to share our family's story, for your love, patience, giving, and for cheering Ali and me on as we wrote, did rewrites, and pulled twelve-hour days. It is true that the best is yet to be. I love you!

From Ali:

I owe my Hansy, my husband, my best friend, my deepest gratitude. You called me your Navy SEAL even when I felt helpless and weak. We have grown up together, we have dreamed dreams together, we have been through each other's darkest hours and are experiencing the brightest days. I love you.

Noah and Luke, for being the light of my life, the joy of my heart, amazing miracles, comic relief, and ever so patient with Mama in the experience of life. Your creativity inspires creativity in me. I love you more than you love me; I said it first.

For my family. Dad, I love being alive and awake alongside you in recovery. Mom, for never quitting on hope, love, and faith. Justin and Chris, it's an honor to be your sister. Tiffany, Maggie, and Erika, you are the sisters I always longed for, your words and encouragement have buoyed me. Mimi, Lynn, and Dru, the amazing Pawhuska Fullers, I'll always be your Pineapple. Cindi and Keith, for all your endless love and support through the years; Jesika and Harrison, I love you so much. I love being neighbors and watching you grow up. Thanks Granny and

Granpa for loving us Plums. Jason, your quiet, immensely creative spirit is inspiring and the "painting gift" will always be appreciated. Caitlin, Caleb, Josephine, and Lucy, you're so creative and beautiful. I love being your aunt. Thanks to the incredible "daughters" and friends who dialogued and shared your stories.

I owe deepest gratitude to Kevin, who helped me find the will to live life through recovery. You showed me how to keep it simple and stay grateful. Kenneth, for listening and showing me what the third step is really about. Thank you to all my friends in recovery. Kathryn, you were my angel and you have been the dearest friend, full of wisdom and unconditional love. Being around you is like being in the shade of a great, strong tree. Sam, thanks for being such an amazing example and friend to the boys. Thanks to Bonnie and Katie, beautiful, talented women. Ruthie, are there even words? You listened and heard us, you helped us find our duet.

Alice and Liz, thank you for finding more in my mom and me than we could see at first. Thank you for encouraging us, listening, and being patient with us in the process. Most of all, thank you to all the mothers who have unconditionally loved us daughters.

NOTES

Chapter One: Letting Go

1. Marilee Zdenek, *Splinters in My Pride* (Santa Barbara, CA: Two Roads Publishing, 2009). First published by Word Books in 1979. Used with permission.
2. Marie Chapian, *Mothers and Daughters: Learning to Be Friends* (Minneapolis: Bethany House, 1988), 175.
3. Christine Proulx, quoted in Kimberly Garza, "Empty Nest," *Spirit* magazine, June 2009, 85.
4. Sharon A. Hersh, *The Last Addiction: Why Self-Help Is Not Enough* (Colorado Springs, CO: WaterBrook Press, 2008), 16.
5. Hersh, *Last Addiction,* 16. (See the Perkinson study at www.robertperkinson.com.)
6. Hersh, *Last Addiction,* 25.
7. Hersh, *Last Addiction,* 148.
8. Hersh, *Last Addiction,* 148.
9. Adapted from Bill P. and Lisa D., *The 12 Step Prayer Book* (Center City, MN: Hazelden, first edition), 37.

Chapter Two: Generational Differences

1. Rosalind C. Barnett, "Adult Daughters and Their Mothers: Harmony or Hostility?" Working Paper Series, No. 209 (Wellesley, MA: Wellesley Centers for Women, 1990), 3.
2. Lisa Selin Davis, "All but the Ring: Why Some Couples Don't Wed," *Time* magazine, May 25, 2009, 57.
3. Barnett, "Adult Daughters and Their Mothers," 3–4.

4. Martha Beck, "Make Your Own Mother," *O, The Oprah Magazine,* May 2003, 259.

Chapter Three: Validating Your Daughter

1. Deborah Tannen, *You're Wearing That? Understanding Mothers and Daughters in Conversation* (New York: Ballantine Books, 2006), 34.
2. Deborah Tannen, "Mom's Unforgiving Mirror," *Washington Post,* April 10, 2007, 1.
3. Harriet Lerner, *The Mother Dance: How Children Change Your Life* (New York: HarperCollins, 1998), 100.
4. From a personal interview with T. Suzanne Eller, author of *The Woman I Am Becoming: Embracing the Chase for Identity, Faith, and Destiny* (Eugene, OR: Harvest House, 2007).
5. Tannen, *You're Wearing That?* 57.

Chapter Four: Too Close for Comfort

1. Leslie Vernick, *The Emotionally Destructive Relationship: Seeing It, Stopping It, Surviving It* (Eugene, OR: Harvest House, 2007), 27–28.

Chapter Five: Respect and Belief

1. Rosalind C. Barnett, "Adult Daughters and Their Mothers: Harmony or Hostility?" Working Paper Series, No. 209 (Wellesley, MA: Wellesley Centers for Women, 1990), 4.

Chapter Six: Communication

1. Deborah Tannen, "The Mother-Daughter Relationship," March 27, 2006, www.gather.com.

2. Rosalind C. Barnett, "Adult Daughters and Their Mothers: Harmony or Hostility?" Working Paper Series, No. 209 (Wellesley, MA: Wellesley Centers for Women, 1990), 3.

3. From an interview with Ruthie Hast, M.Ed., Licensed Professional Counselor, Edmond, Oklahoma.

4. Ann Caron, *Mothers to Daughters* (New York: Henry Holt and Company, 1998), 14–15.

Chapter Seven: Connecting and Bonding

1. Ruth Nemzoff, *Don't Bite Your Tongue: How to Foster Rewarding Relationships with Your Adult Children* (New York: Macmillan, 2008), 167.

Chapter Eight: Are You Going to Church, Honey?

1. Appreciation to Leslie Vernick, licensed therapist and author of *The Emotionally Destructive Relationship*, for sharing her wisdom and insights from her counseling practice and mothering experience.

2. With thanks to Dr. Catherine Hart Weber, psychologist and author of *Is Your Teen Stressed or Depressed? A Practical and Inspirational Guide for Parents of Hurting Teenagers* for her insights on daughters' temperaments and spirituality and her own experience in interviews with the author.

3. Wayne Jacobsen, *He Loves Me! Learning to Live in the Father's Affection* (Newbury Park, CA: Windblown Media, 2007), 183.

Chapter Nine: When Your Daughter Says, "I Do"

1. Sharon Naylor, "My Mother Is Ruining My Wedding," 2009, www.NJWedding.com.

2. Jane Adams, *I'm Still Your Mother: How to Get Along with Your Grown-Up Children for the Rest of Your Life* (New York: Delacorte/Bantam Doubleday Dell, 1994), 103.

3. Naylor, "My Mother Is Ruining My Wedding."

Chapter Eleven: When Crisis Arises

1. O. Hallesby, *Prayer* (Minneapolis: Augsburg, 1994), 23.

2. Hallesby, *Prayer,* 20.

3. Melody Beattie, *Codependent No More: How to Stop Controlling Others and Start Caring for Yourself* (Center City, MN: Hazelden, 1992), 69.

Chapter Thirteen: The Power of Forgiveness

1. *Because I Said So,* directed by Michael Lehmann, Gold Circle Films, 2007.

2. Patti Davis, interview by Lesley Stahl, *CBS Sunday Morning,* CBS, March 29, 2009.

Epilogue

1. Patti Davis, *The Lives Our Mothers Leave Us: Prominent Women Discuss the Complex, Humorous, and Ultimately Loving Relationships They Have with Their Mothers* (Carlsbad, CA: Hay House, 2009), 83.

ABOUT THE AUTHORS

CHERI FULLER is a best-selling, award-winning author, whose overall book sales total more than one million copies. She speaks to a wide range of women as she keynotes at women's conferences, retreats, and events and is a frequent guest on national radio and television programs. Cheri is a contributing writer for *Today's Christian Woman,* and hundreds of her articles have appeared in *Focus on the Family, Family Circle, Better Homes and Gardens, Faith & Spirit, Guideposts, Moody, Marriage Partnership, Decision, ParentLife, Living with Teenagers, Pray!* and other publications.

ALI PLUM is Cheri's daughter, a writer and songwriter, a wife, and a mother to Noah and Luke. She and her mom have weathered the ups and downs of their relationship to find one of the most treasured, honest relationships of their lives. *Mother-Daughter Duet* marks her debut in book publishing.

• • •

We'd love to hear from you!
Connect with Cheri at www.cherifuller.com.
Join Cheri and Ali's blog for discussions, questions, and giveaways at
www.motherdaughterduet.wordpress.com.
Become a friend on Facebook! Search for Cheri Fuller and Ali Plum,
and watch for *Mother-Daughter Duet* on the WaterBrook Multnomah
Facebook fan page.

To invite Cheri or Ali to speak to your group:
visit www.SpeakUpSpeakerServices.com
1-888-870-7719
or e-mail: cheri@cherifuller.com.
aliplum@gmail.com

• • •

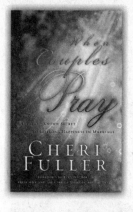

Rediscover the joy of experiencing answered prayer and the fulfillment of deepening marital intimacy as you learn to reignite your prayer life and your relationship.

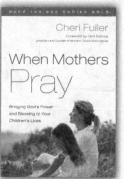

What is the most vital thing a mom can do for her kids? Pray. Find hope, encouragement, and practical advice in this bestseller and discover what happens when mothers pray.

Dare to believe these true stories of God's powerful answers to teens' prayers. *When Teens Pray* helps teenagers learn how they can connect with God and impact the world now by seeing God in prayer.

MULTNOMAH BOOKS